Collins *practical gardener*

GARDEN
TECHNIQUES

Collins *practical gardener*

GARDEN TECHNIQUES

MATTHEW WILSON

First published in 2005 by HarperCollins*Publishers*

77–85 Fulham Palace Road, London, W6 8JB

The Collins website address is:

www.collins.co.uk

Text by Matthew Wilson; copyright © HarperCollins*Publishers*

Artworks and design © HarperCollins*Publishers*

The majority of photographs in this book were taken by
Tim Sandall. A number of other images were supplied
by David Sarton

Cover photography by Tim Sandall

Photographic props: Coolings Nurseries, Rushmore Hill,
Knockholt, Kent, TN14 7NN, www.coolings.co.uk

Design and editorial: Focus Publishing, Sevenoaks, Kent

Project editor: Guy Croton

Editor: Vanessa Townsend

Project co-ordinator: Caroline Watson

Design & illustration: David Etherington

For HarperCollins

Senior managing editor: Angela Newton

Design manager: Luke Griffin

Editor: Alastair Laing

Assistant editor: Lisa John

Production: Chris Gurney

A CIP catalogue record for this book is available from the
British Library

ISBN 0-00-718396-8

Colour reproduction by Colourscan

Printed and bound in Great Britain by The Bath Press Ltd

Contents

Introduction   6

Getting Started   7
Plant Types   24
Tools   56
Planting Techniques   62

Pruning & Maintenance   76
Propagation   89
Growing Plants for Food   96
Greenhouse Gardening   117
Lawns   124
Container Gardening   132
Water Gardening   137

Pests, Diseases & Problems   143
Glossary   155

Index   157
Acknowledgements   160

Introduction

Gardening is generally considered to be the most popular hobby in the developed world, with millions of people across the globe tending 'their patch' with varying degrees of experience and knowledge.

But gardening is much more than just a hobby. It can be a means of artistic expression, a way of improving the environment, and an educational tool for children and adults that brings the natural world and the growth of plants into focus, and helps to show us just how important plants are to the human race. Some gardeners concentrate solely on the ornamental aspects of plants, whilst others value their productivity and grow plants for food. Still others develop a passion for a fairly narrow area of gardening, alpines or woodland plants for example.

This book provides an introduction to the most popular areas of gardening, providing information from plant growth and soil preparation through to pruning and pests. The book has been written with today's gardener in mind, one who is less inclined to use chemicals and more likely to want to encourage wildlife to the garden as part and parcel of the experience and joy of gardening.

Whether you are an experienced gardener looking to increase your knowledge of a different aspect of horticulture, or a novice seeking to learn the fundamental principles of gardening, this book should add to your understanding and enjoyment of gardening.

A well managed garden will give you endless pleasure, whatever its size and nature

Getting Started

Gardening is a vast subject, and to give you some idea, there are almost 100,000 different plants on sale in the UK alone! Imagine trying to learn the names of all of them, or put it another way, imagine trying to learn the names of 100,000 people and then put those names to their faces.

Yet don't feel daunted, because even the most knowledgeable gardener with years of experience won't know every plant name – it is just not possible. However, what a good gardener will have is an understanding of all of the factors that make plants tick and, therefore, make gardens successful. He or she will be able to look at a plant they don't know and at least recognize the family or type of plant it belongs to.

It is this life-long learning that makes gardening so rewarding, because as your knowledge increases so your garden improves. There is nothing dull about gardening, even for those who have done it for years, because the garden scene is ever changing with new plants and techniques being introduced all the time.

So, take your time to learn the basics about gardening because, unlike most things in our fast and furious world, there are no shortcuts in gardening. You are dealing with living things that will decide for themselves how happy they are or not – all you can do is try your best, through learning and experience, to help them along.

Assessing Your Garden

The route to successful gardening lies in understanding your own garden. Gardens can vary widely in size, from a small urban courtyard through suburban plot to a large country garden; in aspect (geographical and topographical location), for example on a windy sunny hilltop or in a sheltered shady valley; in soil type – we will tackle that later – and in microclimate. Without a clear understanding of the unique factors that affect your garden, it is almost impossible to select the right plants or choose the right time to carry out maintenance, planting and so on. Understanding these factors will help to ensure that your gardening experience is a happy and successful one!

Aspect covers the geographical and topographical location of your garden and the direction it faces; north, south, east or west. An open, sunny garden will lend itself to plants that originate from open sunny locations, whilst a shady, sheltered garden will be suitable for an entirely different range of plants – those from shady, sheltered origins!

Along with the prevailing aspect of your garden are more subtle variations in conditions and these are known as microclimates. For example, your garden may be in quite an open and windy location, but the presence of buildings or hedges means that the garden itself is actually quite sheltered and consequently gets very hot in summer. Microclimates can be truly micro, for example: a hot, sunny wall in an otherwise shady garden, or dappled shade at the foot of a deciduous tree in an open site. These microclimates offer plenty of opportunities to try plants that might not be suitable for the greater area of your garden and microclimates can also be manipulated or created to increase the range of plants that you can grow.

There are other really simple ways to assess the prevailing growing conditions in

A sheltered garden will be more suitable for certain groups of plants, such as shade lovers

your neighbourhood. A visit to a public garden can provide valuable information about the types of plants that are suitable for your area and looking at what grows well in neighbouring gardens can also help to influence your choices. But always remember that every garden has its own microclimate, so finding out as much about your own patch really is the starting point for successful gardening.

Aspect

The easiest way to find out which direction your garden faces is to buy or borrow a compass! If, however, you do not have access to one, then simply observe the passage of the sun during the day – is your garden in sun all day, part of the day, or always in shade? Another method is to use a local street map that shows your house and garden. These maps do not usually have north marked on them, but instead are orientated with north at the top of the page. This should give you the information you need to find out the direction in which your garden faces.

In the northern hemisphere, south or south-west facing gardens receive the most sun for the longer part of the day, whilst north facing gardens are mostly in shade and, consequently, cooler. West facing gardens receive the sun in the afternoon, east facing in the morning. In the southern hemisphere the conditions are reversed, with the ideal aspect for maximum sun being north-east facing, where the sun is received for most of the day.

Microclimates

Observation is the key to assessing microclimates. Is there a part of your garden that is always sunny, even when the rest is in shade? This could be suitable for planting with sun loving plants, or perhaps the location of a patio – for sun loving people!

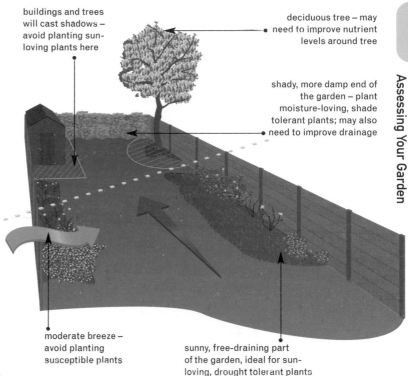

buildings and trees will cast shadows – avoid planting sun-loving plants here

deciduous tree – may need to improve nutrient levels around tree

shady, more damp end of the garden – plant moisture-loving, shade tolerant plants; may also need to improve drainage

moderate breeze – avoid planting susceptible plants

sunny, free-draining part of the garden, ideal for sun-loving, drought tolerant plants

On a windy day, walk around your garden looking for sheltered spots – usually in the lee of a wall or hedge – and also for especially windy areas.

Creating and affecting microclimates

Creating new microclimates within your garden, or altering those that already exist, can open up new opportunities for planting.

Dealing with wind Open, windy gardens can be made more sheltered through the use of screen plantings. Depending on the size of your garden these can range from a hedge right through to a deep 'shelter belt' of trees and shrubs. Solid features such as walls or buildings can create sheltered areas in their immediate vicinity, but they also cause wind turbulence – the wind accelerates over the solid feature and then 'eddies' behind it.

Plants, however, are permeable and consequently the wind passes through them, slowing incrementally without causing turbulence. There are also a range of

Established or uncultivated

The approach you take to your garden is also influenced by its general condition. A mature, established garden may have some key features that you want to retain, while allowing for space to be created to develop new ideas. A neglected garden may look like it needs a clean sweep approach, but be careful, as there may be some hidden gems. A brand new garden offers a clean sheet from which to work, but may well be hindered by poor soil and buried rubbish – often the case when a new house is built. In all cases, it is worth taking a little time, deciding what you want from your garden and setting it down on paper. Visiting other gardens and gardening shows, and reading a few books on garden design will go a long way towards helping you establish your dream garden.

Improve light levels in a shady garden by crown lifting. This is achieved by pruning the lower branches – not only of trees, but also large shrubs

windbreak products available, usually taking the form of a woven netting which, when fixed to posts, acts in the same way as a hedge, shielding plants to great effect.

A combination of windbreak netting and hedge planting can be especially effective in a really exposed garden, as the netting will create a microclimate for the hedge which, in turn, will establish more quickly and help to shelter the garden. In a really exposed garden it may be worth considering planting hedges inside the garden as well, creating a series of 'garden rooms' that are progressively more sheltered.

Dealing with shade In a shady garden, light levels can be improved by painting walls with light colours to reflect sunlight, and by pruning the lower branches of trees and shrubs – this is called crown lifting – or thinning out branches. This will increase the amount of light reaching the soil.

Garden Styles

What makes gardening today so exciting is that it is accessible to so many people. In the past only the wealthy and landed could afford to maintain ornamental gardens, whereas today anyone with a garden can let their imagination go and create an outdoor space that is suitable for their own needs. One consequence of this mass participation in gardening is that there is no single style dominating taste or design, unlike the defined fashions of the past such as the Picturesque or Landscape Movements, which dominated the 1700s.

The Modern Ornamental Garden

The modern ornamental garden can be whatever the owner wants it to be; a chic, low-input courtyard featuring strong architectural plants – or no plants at all – a practical space for a family to play and relax in, or a highly decorative 'plantsman's' garden. And all stages in-between!

With the rich history of garden design to draw from, it is also possible to take elements from past styles, or create a modern interpretation of a garden from another era. In recent years, numerous festivals of garden design have been established, where new and innovative approaches to the use of outdoor space are explored by leading designers.

At the cutting edge

The absence of a predominant style of garden design makes this an exciting time for gardeners and designers. Some of the most interesting and challenging new ideas can be found at design festivals and flower shows, such as at The Reford Gardens, Quebec, Canada, The Festival of Garden Design at Chaumont sur Loire, France, and the RHS Chelsea Flower Show, UK. Gardening magazines frequently cover design issues and garden design is, increasingly, the subject of television programmes. Tapping in to some of these resources will help to provide plenty of inspiration.

Garden designers are not necessarily constrained by the need to use flowering plants and this has led to creations such as Fernando Caruncho's Wheat Parterre in Catalonia – where the 17th century fashion for formal, block planting surrounded by low, clipped hedges has been reinvented using wheat and mown grass – Charles Jenks's DNA and Physics Garden in Scotland, featuring sculptural earth mounds clothed in close mown turf, and the Lower Central Garden at the Getty Centre, Los Angeles, designed by Robert Irwin. All of these gardens utilize modern materials, new ideas for planting and innovative approaches to the relationship between gardens and the surrounding landscape.

Cottage Style Gardens

To many, the cottage garden is the epitome of the traditional floral garden, most often associated with the UK and especially England. But the original cottage gardens were not developed as part of a garden design trend, but out of necessity. Cottage gardens were places where a combination of fruit, vegetables, herbs and flowers could be grown, but there was no sentiment attached to cultivating these plants – they all had to pay for their space. Fruit and vegetables were grown for food, supplementing the diets of the cottagers who were often poorly paid agricultural workers or craftspeople.

The dense mixed plantings of a classic English cottage garden represent a popular view of what defines a garden

Cottage garden plants

It is the choice of plants that really give a cottage garden its unique flavour. Apart from edible crops such as peas, runner beans, lettuce and onions, some of the most popular and enduring cottage garden plants are flowering perennials and annuals. Those that are still commonly grown today include:

Hollyhock (*Alcea rosea*)
English marigold (*Calendula officinalis*)
Delphinium (*Delphinium* Belladonna group and *D.* Elatum group)
Dame's Violet (*Hesperis matronalis*)
Lavender (*Lavendula angustifolia*)

Herbs were harvested in these gardens to flavour food or to hang to keep out flies – which have a particular aversion to lavender – and flowers were there for cutting, but also to attract the insects needed to pollinate the productive crops and protect them from insect pests. Every bit of the cottage garden produced something edible or useful – the fact that the mixed plantings often looked idyllic and defined many people's view of what a garden should look like was purely coincidental.

The layout of a cottage garden is very much dictated by the site, but common materials include brick or gravel paths, stone or brick border edges and lawns that are either small or completely omitted – lawns of course are not productive but labour intensive.

The attraction of the cottage garden style to the modern gardener is that the emphasis is very much on the informal use of plants, creating a soft, almost 'olde worlde' feel. The fact that productive plants can be incorporated in an ornamental planting is a bonus, as it enables the cottage gardener to enjoy both the visual and edible aspects of the garden, in a way that is horticulturally complementary and visually appealing.

Formal Ornamental Garden

Formality – the laying out of a garden according to defined principles and, usually, geometric forms – has always existed in gardens. Ancient Roman gardens – which are amongst the first for which we have sound archaeological evidence – were frequently rectangular in shape, usually attached to the

Grandiose formal gardens have been symbols of wealth and status for centuries

house by a terrace and enclosed by hedges of laurel, box or yew. Within this rectangle, geometry played a key role, the use of straight lines, right-angles and sections of circles being the norm. The Moorish gardens of The Alhambra Palace and Generalife in Spain combined formality with religious significance, whilst later European gardens continued the theme, with topiary, parterres and knot gardens, mazes and the like all playing a part in garden design until the rise of the Picturesque and Landscape movements of the 1700s. These new, natural styles sought to recreate romantic, idealized landscapes by 'improving' on nature.

Formal ornamental garden features

The key features of formal gardens include:

• Hedges, usually of box (*Buxus sempervirens*), yew (*Taxus baccata*), beech (*Fagus sylvatica*) or hornbeam (*Carpinus betulus*), all of which are closely clipped.
• Water features, fountains and cascades.
• Straight lines and geometric divisions.
• Large block plantings – such as traditional rose gardens and bedding schemes – or an absence of plants in favour of closely managed green space comprised of grass and hedges.
• Topiary, which is the creation of 'living sculpture' made from clipped box and yew.
• Statuary, urns and containers.

By the time of the Victorian era, formality was back in vogue once again as gardening embarked on a journey into what can now be referred to as 'high horticulture' – labour-intensive plantings such as carpet bedding, formal rose gardens and the resurrection of the garden parterre.

The design principles behind formal gardens are still applicable today and are often revisited and reinvented in modern designs. In a small space, creating distinct divisions, often referred to as garden rooms, can lead to a feeling of greater space and a sense of transition from one place to another. The use of a strong formal design can also give a real sense of purpose to a garden, however large or small it might be.

The Productive Garden

In the past, the production of food on a small scale was a matter of necessity rather than of choice. The medieval peasantry supplemented their diets by growing a range of edible crops on small plots of land in a form of subsistence farming. The presence of edible plants in gardens has waxed and waned ever since, depending on socio-economic conditions, so in times of shortage – such as in Europe during the Second World War – there has been a major increase in the growing of edible plants, usually at the expense of ornamental gardening which, understandably at the time, was seen as superfluous.

A productive garden can also be a stylish garden, as demonstrated by this carefully trained and cultivated apple tree

Productive gardening is, arguably, the most labour-intensive form of gardening and the one requiring the greatest attention to detail. This is because the cultural requirements of edible plants require greater manipulation than most ornamental plants and timing is everything. So, for example, soil cultivation, fertilizing, sowing, irrigation and so on are often more time-sensitive than with ornamentals.

The advantages of growing your own food are simple: fresh produce on your table that you can eat with absolute confidence knowing that you have controlled the growing environment. With the increasing interest in organic food, producing your own at home has to be a good choice. Having a large garden to grow it in is not necessarily a requirement, as allotments are available in most areas. These publicly owned open spaces, established specifically for small scale productive horticulture, can be rented – usually from a local authority – for a comparatively small amount, which will quickly be repaid in fresh, delicious food.

Naturalistic & Wildlife Gardens

In recent years there has been a widespread move toward more naturalistic gardens and especially those that are designed and maintained with wildlife in mind.

Naturalistic gardens are precisely that; the design and plant content are influenced by natural plant communities and

Wildflower meadows need not be large and offer a low-maintenance method of introducing new plants

ecosystems and then interpreted in an ornamental setting. This style of gardening offers the opportunity to garden with minimal intervention, as the plants that you grow are naturally suited to the prevailing conditions and consequently involve less maintenance than more conventional plantings.

Wildlife gardens are often misrepresented as needing to be untidy and unkempt. In fact, any garden that has plants in it has some value to wildlife, and it is more a matter of plant selection and

10 ways to make your garden more wildlife friendly

- Put up bird feeders and keep them filled right throughout the year.
- Carefully site bird nest boxes in your garden and bat boxes too. Remember to clean them out during winter, before the new breeding season.
- Choose plants that are pollen and nectar rich, produce berries, fruits or nuts, or are a natural food source for invertebrate larvae. Remember, some 'highly bred' cultivars are sterile and of no benefit to wildlife.
- Include some native plants if possible, providing they are not invasive weeds.
- An old log pile or standing decaying wood will provide food and shelter for invertebrates, which in turn will be predated by higher animals.
- Include a water feature. This could be a full-scale pond or a small, shallow pool. Water is a must-have ingredient in a wildlife garden.
- Leave perennials and grasses standing through winter and cut them down in spring, rather than autumn. This will provide food and shelter for a wide range of animals – and will look good, too!
- Do not use chemical pest controls. Not only do you risk harming beneficial wildlife, you will also remove the food source from those beneficial animals and unbalance your garden.
- Leave an area of long grass for amphibians and moth larvae.
- Be sure not to cut hedges during the bird nesting season, as this can cause the parents to abandon the nest.

A garden that attracts wildlife enjoys many different benefits

maintenance than design that will influence just how wildlife friendly a garden can be. There are some very practical reasons for encouraging wildlife into your garden, as a well balanced garden is less prone to pest outbreaks – the presence of beneficial insects, birds, mammals and amphibians help to control plant pest. Not only that, a garden full of wildlife will bring you as much pleasure as the plants within it.

Understanding Soil

For the vast majority of garden plants soil is all important, providing anchorage, nutrients and the primary source of moisture. Soils vary widely, as do methods of cultivation and improvement, so a good understanding of the soil in your garden is vital.

The composition of most well-cultivated soils is:

- **50–60% mineral matter** – the result of the erosion and weathering of rock.

- **5% organic matter** – decomposed or decomposing organic material, such as leaves, manure, garden compost and so on.

- **35–45% air and water** – these are vital for plant growth and make up the pore space in the soil of your garden.

The topsoil is most associated with plant growth, and underlying it is subsoil.

Identifying your soil type

The size and type of mineral particles in soil largely determines the type and texture of the soil. Particles range from the smallest, which is sand, through clay, silt and stones/gravel. The simplest way to test your soil texture is by using a 'feel test' (see below).

The feel test

Take a handful of soil from your garden, wet it with water then try to roll it into a ball. Rub a little of the wetted soil between your thumb and forefinger and you will be able to feel the particles that are present. Depending on what happens the following will apply:

- If the soil feels 'gritty' and will not roll into a ball, it is a sandy soil.
- If it feels a little gritty, rolls into a ball but soon crumbles apart, it is a sandy loam.
- Loam soil rolls readily into a ball and has no grittiness.
- Clay loams are easy to roll into a ball and when rubbed between thumb and forefinger take a noticeable shine.
- A clay soil will mould into a ball that will be hard to deform. They are sticky and when rubbed polish easily.

How to Improve Your Soil

Whatever the particular characteristics of the soil in your garden, there are various techniques for cultivating it to help improve the structure, nutrient levels and drainage, leading to better plant establishment and growth.

Digging over

Double digging is a soil cultivation technique suitable for soils that have a very good depth of topsoil or are light or thin (see instructions below).

Single digging follows exactly the same process as double digging, except the trenches are just one spit deep. This technique is more suited to soils that have less deep topsoil.

Adding Organic Matter

Organic matter is added to soil in order to improve its structure, drainage and nutrient levels. Apply it to the surface and gently fork into the soil, or, when starting a border from scratch, add it at the digging over stage. This will ensure a rich, well balanced soil that will benefit plants from the outset.

Farmyard manure can improve soil structure and boost nutrient levels, but must have been allowed to rot for at least a year as fresh manure can kill plants. Heavy manures are less suitable on heavy soils, especially clay, where they can bind the soil together even more.

Garden compost improves structure, nutrient levels and often drainage potential. It is produces by composting green waste in the garden (see Making Compost, opposite).

Dig in organic matter to raise nutrient levels and improve the structure of the soil

1 – To double dig a border, for example, dig a trench two to three spits wide and two spits deep (a spit is the length of the head of a spade, that is, the bit that does the digging) across the width of the border. Place the soil to one side.

2 – Into the base of the trench add organic matter to a depth of one spit.

3 – Now dig a second trench alongside the first, placing the soil from this trench on top of the organic matter in the first trench, and repeat the process right along the whole border.

4 – Finally, place the soil from the very first trench you dug (step 1, above) on top of the organic matter in the last trench, to complete the process. You may need to make use of a wheelbarrow in order to transport the soil from the first trench into the last.

1

2

3

4

TIP Timing is all important with soil cultivation: the soil should not be frozen or waterlogged and should be easy to work.

Composted bark adds structure and improves drainage, especially on heavy soils, but has little nutrient value.

Leaf litter is an excellent soil improver, aiding structure and drainage and adding a degree of nutrition.

Hops and mushroom compost If you can find them, spent hops and mushroom compost are effective, lightweight soil improvers – but they can affect soil pH.

Mulching

Mulching is the application of a surface dressing of organic or inorganic matter to control weeds, aid moisture retention and, depending on the type of mulch, to improve soil structure and nutrient levels.
• Apply mulches when the soil is beginning to warm up and has good moisture levels, and this is usually the case in mid- to late spring.
• Do not mulch when the soil is frozen, waterlogged or very dry.
• Do not mulch over the crowns (growing points) of perennials or the 'neck' of woody plants where the stem meets the ground, as this can cause rotting.

Making Compost

Composting is the recycling of green waste into a usable soil improver or mulch for the garden – it is totally organic and 100% free!

What to add:
• Grass clippings
• Vegetable peelings
• Spent stems from perennials
• Thin woody material (less than 10mm/¼in)
• Annual weeds
• Spent annual plants and bedding plants

A ready supply of well rotted compost will make your gardening life easier and more fulfilling

• Fallen leaves
• Old turf and topsoil
• Hedge clippings
• Spent potting compost
• Manure

What NOT to add:
• Perennial weeds
• Meat products
• Diseased material
• Inorganic matter such as plastics or metal

Steps to compost success

The traditional compost heap is arguably the best, providing it is set up and managed properly. Here is how to establish one:

• Choose a site in full sun or light shade.
• Make a 'bin' 2 x 2m (6 x 6ft) square and around 1.4m (5ft) high from timber or old pallet, open at the front or with a removable section, and with a floor of bare earth.
• Start off with a layer of grass clippings or perennial stems to a depth of 20–40cm (8–16in). Add a second layer, of fallen leaves or spent bedding plants, and so on.
• Once you start to see decomposition and heat generated, monitor the heap to make sure it does not become excessively dry or overly wet. Turn the compost regularly with a fork. The compost should be ready to use after eight months to a year.

Using Fertilizers

Fertilizers are either inorganic synthesized compounds or naturally occurring organic compounds that improve the nutrient and mineral levels of soils.

What's in a fertilizer?

The three primary nutrients found in plant fertilisers are:
• Nitrogen (N) – for green growth
• Phosphorus (P) – for flowers
• Potassium (K) – for root growth

In addition to these there are a number of other nutrients and essential minerals, equally important to plant growth.

Compound fertilizers supply two or more of the main nutrients for plant growth. They have the advantage of being designed for specific tasks, such as improving root structure or boosting green growth.

Straight fertilizers supply only one nutrient in concentrated form. These are designed for a specific requirement, such as boosting flowering in tomatoes, and should not be used as a general feed.

Both compound and straight fertilizers can be applied as either a surface dressing of granules, in liquid feeds or as crushed material such as bonemeal.

Soil Characteristics

Sandy soils

Sandy soils are free draining, quick to warm in spring and easy to cultivate, ideal for plants that come from hot, dry environments. However, they do not hold water well and nutrients often wash through the topsoil. Erosion can be a problem, especially on exposed sites.

Sandy soils will benefit from:
• Regular improvement with organic matter in spring and autumn.
• Annual mulching with an organic mulch.
• Inclusion of water retaining granules when planting, which may help establish larger, woody plants.
• Application of fertilizers.

Loam soils

A deep loam soil is probably the ideal soil for gardening. They tend to be fertile, well drained yet moisture retentive, easy to cultivate and suitable for growing most plants. But they are not without their problems: over cultivation can lead to panning, where a hard layer of soil forms under the surface that can act as a barrier to plant roots, and especially capping – where rainfall causes the surface soil to bind

There are numerous fertilizers and plant feeds available on the market, but do not over use them

TIP

It is tempting to simply apply fertilizers as a matter of course, but over-enrichment can encourage soft, sappy growth in plants that is then prone to pests and diseases and will require extra watering. Good soil cultivation is the primary route to healthy plant growth.

together, preventing water from penetrating the surface.

Loam soils will benefit from:
• Regular (spring and autumn) improvement with organic matter.
• Annual mulching, to alleviate capping.
• Changing the depth of cultivation, to reduce the risk of panning.
• Application of fertilizers.

Chalk soils

Chalk soils share some characteristics with sandy soils, but are variable depending on whether the chalk is mixed with loam or clay, and how close to the surface the chalk is. The most important aspect of chalk soils relates to pH (see box below) as they tend to be alkaline.

Clay soils

Clay soils are a challenge! Though fertile, they tend to be hard to cultivate, poorly drained and prone to panning and compaction – in summer they can bake as hard as concrete, while in winter they can turn into a quagmire. However, clay soils can be won over, providing the appropriate cultivation methods are applied and, above all, the timing is right.

Clay soils will benefit from:
• Annual incorporation of sandy grit, applied to a depth of 10cm (4in) and then worked in with a fork.
• Annual improvement with lightweight organic matter – leafmould, composted bark and garden compost are ideal.
• Annual mulching.
• Variation of the depth of cultivation.
• Application of fertilizers.

Silt soils

Silt soils are often fertile but can be difficult to cultivate as they tend to behave like sandy soils. They are very prone to capping as the soil particles are so fine, and can also be prone to compaction and erosion. Silt soils hold water well but can often dry out at the surface, which can be problematic when growing plants from seed.

Silt soils will benefit from:
• Regular (spring and autumn) improvement of borders with organic matter, by single or double digging.
• Annual mulching.
• Surface incorporation of lightweight organic matter, to prevent capping and improve surface moisture.
• Application of fertilizers.

Whatever kind of soil you have, work at improving it – it will be worth it in the long run!

The importance of pH

The pH scale is a means of measuring the acidity or alkalinity of soil. Neutral is expressed as 7 on the pH scale and values below that denote an acid soil, whilst above that means the soil is alkaline. The ideal pH for most plants is slightly acid at 6.5, but there are a range of plants for all soil pH levels. Testing your soil pH is easy, with tester kits available from garden shops. Attempting to grow acid-loving plants such as rhododendrons in alkaline soil will almost always result in failure, so knowing the pH of your soil is vital.

How Plants Grow

An understanding of how plants grow will contribute greatly to making sure that your garden is full of healthy, happy plants that grow and flower well and are more resilient to climatic changes and resistant to pests and diseases. Plants are no different from humans in that they, like us, have particular requirements in order for them to be healthy and grow well. Remove or reduce one of the components that are key to plant growth and, just as would be the case with us, the health of the plant suffers.

Many of the components that are essential to plant growth are the same as those required for good human health – unsurprisingly given that green plants are such a key part of a healthy human diet. These components are:

• Water
• Air (primarily carbon dioxide)
• Nutrients and minerals
• Light

Plant Anatomy

Although the plant kingdom is hugely diverse, the 'average' garden plant – if there

A healthy root structure is vital to a plant's long term prospects and chances of survival

is such a thing – is comprised of the following parts that make up a recognizable whole:

• Root system
• Stem
• Leaves
• Flower structure

Root Systems

The root system enables a plant to take up water, nutrients and minerals, also providing anchorage either to the soil or, in the case of epiphytes (air plants), to another plant. Root systems vary widely as a consequence of the ability of plants to adapt to specific conditions – we will cover this in a later chapter – and it is worth understanding what the root system of a particular plant is like before planting it. Here are some examples:

Tap roots These are long, tapering roots that extend down into the soil, and if you asked a child to draw a root, this is probably what you would get. Classic tap-rooted plants include carrots and parsnips, but there are many ornamental plants with tap roots, too, such as *Eryngium giganteum*.

Fibrous roots These refer to a network of fine feeder roots attached to more substantial roots that help to anchor the plant. Often a fibrous root system will be very close to or even at soil level, so soil disturbance can often be very damaging to such plants. Fibrous root systems are often extensive. Imagine a large forest tree, with a big canopy of branches: the root system of such a tree will extend up to a third again beyond the reach of the branches. Plants with fibrous root systems include lavender, Malus (apple) and Rhododendron.

Bulbs, corms and tubers These are all root adaptations, existing primarily to help the plant to store energy in the form of starch. Often these plants have a comparatively brief period

Bulbs are adaptations of root systems, designed to store nutrients which are then released to the plant

of growth and flower and then spend many months 'at rest', hence the need to store energy. For example, daffodil, crocus, cyclamen and *Geranium tuberosum*, which flower in spring and then disappear completely during summer. The best known tuberous rooted plant is probably the 'noble tuber', the potato.

Rhizomatous roots Rhizomes are often fleshy and starchy, like tuberous roots. Plants with root systems such as this often use the roots as a means of spreading and some can be quite invasive, which is good for covering a large space but less helpful in a small garden. Plants with rhizomatous roots include bearded iris (non-spreading) and Japanese anemone (*Anemone x hybrida*), which spreads but is not invasive.

Stems

The stem supports the parts of the plant that, in gardening terms, make it worth having – flowers and foliage. As well as supporting these structures, the stem also has many other roles to play in the life of the plant, including the transportation of food, water and minerals around the plant. These movements take place through vascular tissues collectively known as vascular bundles, comprised of the xylem and phloem. Think of these as a road system delivering goods from one part of the plant to the other. The xylem enables

TIP

Protecting the stem of the plant is crucial. This might take the form of protection from animals or machinery, for example by using stem guards or fencing off vulnerable plants, or could simply be a case of ensuring that tall herbaceous plants are staked to prevent them from being damaged or snapping off in strong winds.

the transportation of water and minerals around the plant, whilst the phloem delivers the food manufactured in the leaves to other parts of the plant. These vascular bundles are very close to the outer surface or skin of the stem (the epidermis) and are vulnerable should this outer surface be damaged. When trees have their bark stripped from around the trunk – known as ring barking – they usually die, for exactly this reason, as the vascular bundles have been damaged and the plant can no longer feed itself.

The tip of the stem is also the main growing point for plants – the reason they grow upwards rather than sideways or downwards. This phenomenon is usually referred to as apical dominance, and is why 'pinching out' the growing tip of a plant helps to make it bushier, by temporarily removing the dominant cells. It is also the reason why many plants flower and fruit better when trained horizontally – climbing roses and fruiting vines, for example – as they put more effort into their lateral growth than their apical growth: growing out and producing flowers and fruit rather than simply growing up and up.

The stem of a plant controls the distribution of the water and minerals it needs to survive

Leaves

Leaves perform a number of vital functions for plants, as this is where the majority of food production and respiration takes place. Plants produce food through photosynthesis using minerals and water drawn up by the roots, light absorbed through the leaf surface and carbon dioxide diffused into the leaf through the process of respiration. A by-product of photosynthesis – during daylight hours – is oxygen, which is why plants are vitally important to the health of the earth and are often referred to as the 'lungs of the earth'. In order to absorb the maximum amount of light possible and thereby photosynthesize efficiently, the plant uses minerals to produce a pigment called chlorophyll, and it is this that gives plants their green coloration and is why yellowing leaves are a good indicator of plant sickness.

There are also a range of plants with leaves that are coloured other than green. Many of these, such as *Cotinus* 'Grace' are amongst the most useful of garden plants, as they can bring a different dimension to a planting scheme and create colour through foliage as well as flower. However, beneath the surface these plants are still green – it is the presence of a masking chemical that 'hides' the chlorophyll and makes the plant appear a different colour. There are also plants with leaves that appear a different

A substance named chlorophyll – produced by photosynthesis – gives the leaves of plants their green colour

Variegated and coloured leaves

Plants with bi-coloured, patterned leaves – referred to as variegated leaves - are often attractive additions to the garden. Variegation is an irregular arrangement of pigment in the leaves and usually occurs as a result of a mutation, but sometimes as a consequence of disease. Plant breeders have taken advantage of these occurrences and variegated plants are now a common component in many gardens.

colour due to their external structure, namely the presence of fine hairs that tend to make the plant look silver or grey.

Flowers

The beauty of flowers is one of the main reasons for growing plants in the first place. However, plants do not produce beautiful blooms for our benefit and this is borne out by the number of species that bear nondescript, inconspicuous flowers. They are, of course, designed to attract pollinators – insects, birds and animals – and different plants have developed different strategies to ensure that they get the right pollinator at the right time. Here are a couple of examples:

This *Cornus kousa* is a good example of a plant that bears bracts to attract pollinating insects

Flowers of cultivated plants

Cultivated plants – known as 'cultivars', an abbreviation of cultivated varieties – are those that have been 'created' by plant breeders. This is achieved by carrying out cross pollination in a controlled environment between known parent plants and then monitoring the subsequent seedlings for notable or 'garden worthy' traits. These can include flower colour, size and shape or factors such as resistance to disease, size or growth habit, and so on. In a few instances the pursuit of these new characteristics can result in the flowers being sterile, producing no pollen or nectar. This is worth bearing in mind if you want to attract wildlife to your garden, and a good nursery or garden centre will be able to advise you on those plants that are sterile.

• *Cornus kousa* (flowering dogwood) bears small, button like flowers in spring. On their own they would be unlikely to attract much at all, so at flowering time the flowers are surrounded by leaves that are modified to look like large petals, known as bracts. These make a much bigger show, enough to attract pollinating insects and make *C. kousa* a very attractive garden plant.
• *Chimonanthus praecox* flowers in winter when there are few insect pollinators around. So, in order to attract those that are about it has highly fragrant flowers. The scent travels a long distance – even by our standards – it is an act of survival of the smelliest that makes it, and many other winter flowering plants, very welcome in the ornamental garden.

The reason these measures are taken is simple. Plants need to procreate, and in order to do so their flowers need to be pollinated so that they can develop seeds that will grow into new plants.

Seeds

Successful pollination results in the development of seeds, one of the primary means by which plants propagate. Surrounding the seed is a protective layer – the fruit – which is often edible, not least to us humans. The advantage of this to the plant is that in consuming the fruit the bird or animal responsible becomes a dispersal system for the seed, carrying it away from the mother plant and then depositing it, along with some fresh manure in the form of droppings. Other seeds have no need for a fruit layer as they are dispersed by wind – think of dandelions – water, or, in the case of plants like the Californian poppy (*Eschscholzia californica*) by a miniature explosion, caused by the seed pod drying out and then bursting open with enough force to make an audible 'crack'.

The wide, tubular flowers of Digitalis are specially designed to allow easy access to bumblebees

Plant Types

Over the next few pages we will look at the overriding factor that makes gardening so exciting, life affirming and, above all, rewarding – the plants themselves. For most of us, plants are the reason why we garden, and the pleasure gained from watching a plant grow and flourish is hard to convey to people who do not share the passion. Experiencing this pleasure is also the reason why it is worth taking the time to understand more about your garden and its soil and aspect, and learning about how and why plants grow and the conditions they respond to. Why? Because armed with that understanding we can avoid the disappointment of seeing cherished plants fade and die, which can be costly as well as frustrating.

What's in a name?
Plant names are comprised of the following elements:
• The family (not usually used in practical situations)
• The genus
• The species
• The cultivar, variety or subspecies

To get a better understanding of how this works let me relate myself to a plant – *Rosa banksiae* 'Lutea'. First is the extended family, cousins, second cousins, uncles and aunts; in my case the Wilsons, Bacons, etc, and this is just the same as an extended plant family, Rosaceae in our example. Next is the genus, that is, the branch of my family to which I belong, Wilson – Rosa. Then comes the species – *matthew, banksiae*. Finally, if I was to be hybridized and the hybrid had distinctively different characteristics to me, blue hair for example, that hybrid would be named thus:

Wilson (Family) *Wilson* (Genus) *matthew* (Species)
'Blue Hair' (Cultivar)
Or in the case of our rose:
Rosaceae (Family) *Rosa* (Genus) *banksiae* (Species)
'Lutea' (Cultivar)

The use of italics for genus and species is deliberate, while cultivars are always shown in quotation marks and not italicized.

Broad Leaved Trees

Broad leaved trees must be among the most evocative of all plants. Think of a woodland in early summer, a stately avenue of mature specimens, or a broad spreading specimen tree in an open landscape, and then try to imagine being without them. The term 'broad leaved' distinguishes this group of plants from coniferous trees, which generally have thin, needle like leaves. Whilst there are few gardens large enough for broad leaved forest trees, there is a range of excellent smaller trees suitable for almost every garden.

Broad leaved trees make an excellent focal point in the garden, are useful as screening plants or for creating a shady area in a hot garden, and can bring flower, fruit, autumn colour and bark interest. Plant them as solitary specimens, as part of a mixed border to provide permanent structure to the design, or in groups where an underplanting of spring bulbs can make a highly effective combination.

Acer cappadocicum 'Aureum'

Acer cappadocicum 'Aureum' produces bright yellow leaves in spring that gradually turn green in summer, before an autumn display of yellow once more.

Height and spread:	15 x 10m (49 x 32ft)
Flower colour:	Pale yellow, in umbels
Cultivation requirements:	Fertile, moist but well drained soil. As this is a plant with yellow leaves it needs a sheltered spot, as wind and exposure can cause scorching of the leaves
Flowering time:	Early summer
Place of origin:	Garden origin
Suitable for:	Planting as a specimen tree

Betula utilis var. jacquemontii

Betula utilis var. *Jacquemontii* is primarily grown for its beautiful ghostly white bark, which peels away in flakes, and its light and airy foliage. As bark effect is the primary reason to grow this tree, it is worth planting as a multi-stemmed plant, thereby maximizing the effect.

Height and spread:	18 x 10m (59 x 32ft)
Flower colour:	Produces yellowish brown male catkins
Cultivation requirements:	Moderately fertile, moist but well drained soil. Full sun to partial shade
Flowering time:	During early spring
Place of origin:	Himalayas
Suitable for:	As a specimen tree, especially against a dark background such as a hedge, or as part of a winter garden planting in a mixed border. Also very effective planted in groups of three or more.

Crataegus laevigata 'Rosea Flora Pleno'

Crataegus laevigata 'Rosea Flora Pleno' is a beautiful small tree with a mouthful of a name! It has small, glossy, lobed leaves and comes equipped with thorns – it is a type of hawthorn – and a rounded habit. The fragrance of hawthorn flowers is something of an acquired taste, with some people likening them to the smell of cats.

Height and spread:	8 x 8m (26 x 26ft)
Flower colour:	Pink, double flowers, followed by small red fruit
Cultivation requirements:	Any soil in full sun to partial shade
Flowering time:	Late spring
Place of origin:	Garden origin
Suitable for:	This is a robust and adaptable tree suitable for many uses and particularly tolerant of exposed sites.

Malus 'Evereste'

Malus 'Evereste' is a highly decorative ornamental crab apple, with red buds opening to white blossom in spring and orange/red, spherical fruit in autumn that persist well into winter.

Height and spread:	7 x 6m (23 x 20ft)
Flower colour:	White
Cultivation requirements:	Moderately fertile, moist but well drained soil in an open sunny site, although some shade is tolerated
Flowering time:	Spring
Place of origin:	Garden origin
Suitable for:	Crab apples are excellent specimen plants, suitable for smaller gardens and particularly good for attracting wildlife

Robinia pseudoacacia 'Frisia'

Robinia pseudoacacia 'Frisia' has pea-like, pinnate foliage that is golden yellow in spring, becoming more green in summer and then turning yellow again in autumn.

Height and spread:	5 x 8m (16 x 26ft)
Flower colour:	White
Cultivation requirements:	Moderately fertile, moist but well drained soil in full sun, although robinias will cope with poor, droughty soils
Flowering time:	Early to mid-summer
Place of origin:	Garden origin
Suitable for:	As a specimen tree, robinias have very brittle wood, making them unsuitable for exposed sites or where falling limbs may cause damage – this is not a tree for planting on the street or near to where cars are parked!

Sorbus aucuparia

Sorbus aucuparia is a graceful tree with pinnate leaves that display an excellent autumn colour, either red or more often, yellow. Umbels of flowers in spring are followed by clusters of orange/red berries, which are often eaten by birds before the autumn. Rowan is the common name for this tree.

Height and spread:	15 x 7m (49 x 226ft)
Flower colour:	White
Cultivation requirements:	Moist but well drained, neutral to acid soil, ideally humus rich. Will tolerate full sun to dappled shade
Flowering time:	Spring
Place of origin:	Europe/Asia
Suitable for:	As a specimen, in a mixed border, a wild garden or as part of a group planting of trees. Sorbus are particularly tolerant of pollution, making them especially suitable for urban planting

Conifers

Conifers range from massive forest trees right down to tiny, compact shrubby trees. This is a record breaking group of plants that includes some of the tallest trees on earth – *Sequoia sempervirens*, the coastal redwood – the heaviest trees, the giant redwood *Sequoiadendron giganteum*, and arguably, the oldest trees on earth, *Pinus aristata*, the bristle cone pine.

The history of conifers and gardens has been mixed, with popularity coming and going, but conifers are actually extremely useful, versatile plants, the dwarf and compact forms making the perfect foil for ornamental grasses and stem colour plants, whilst the larger trees provide impact and presence in the garden throughout the year.

Picea orientalis 'Aurea'

Picea orientalis 'Aurea' is a large conical to columnar tree with attractive pink-grey bark. For six weeks or so in spring this form has creamy yellow new foliage.

Height and spread:	30 x 8m (98 x 26ft)
Cultivation requirements:	Deep, moist but well drained soil, ideally neutral to acid soil in full sun
Place of origin:	Garden origin
Suitable for:	As a specimen tree in a large garden

Abies koreana

Abies koreana is a small, conical tree with shiny, dark green needles that are silver beneath. These contrast beautifully with the violet-blue cones that it produces in spring.

Height and spread:	10 x 6m (33 x 20ft)
Cultivation requirements:	Neutral to slightly acid soil that is moist but well drained, *A. koreana* will enjoy a sunny position and benefit from shelter from cold winds
Place of origin:	Southern Korea
Suitable for:	Ideal as a specimen tree

Pinus mujo 'Ophir'

Pinus mujo 'Ophir' is a golden form of the dwarf mountain pine. Slow growing and compact, it has sticky resinous buds and attractive foliage.

Height and spread:	3 x 4m (10 x 13ft)
Cultivation requirements:	Well drained soil in full sun. *P. mujo* 'Ophir' is drought tolerant
Place of origin:	Garden origin
Suitable for:	An excellent architectural plant suitable for a dry gravel garden, as a specimen in a border or with ornamental grasses and bulbs

Taxus baccata 'Fastigiata'

Taxus baccata 'Fastigiata' is an erect, fastigiate form of the common yew, commonly known as the Irish yew. It is somewhat slower growing than *T. baccata*.

Height and spread:	10 x 6m (33 x 20ft)
Cultivation requirements:	In the wild, yews are capable of growing out of pure chalk or in crevices in limestone rock. Therefore good drainage and alkaline soil are essential
Place of origin:	Garden origin
Suitable for:	As an architectural punctuation mark, or planted in rows as a strong vertical accent in a formal garden

Shrubs

Shrubs are defined as being 'woody' perennials with a permanent structure above ground that, unlike herbaceous perennials, does not die down in winter. Shrubs are a broad and versatile group of plants, with some that are grown primarily for their flowers but many others that are cultivated for bark effect, foliage colour, berries or fruits and so on.

In most gardens it is the shrubby element of the planting that provides a permanent presence throughout the seasons, providing a backdrop for the 'flashier' herbaceous perennials or annual plants. Shrubs can be grown in groups for a massed effect, as individual specimens surrounded by low growing perennials or in grass, or used as accent points in a mixed border.

Although they are often thought of as being large plants, there is a vast array of shrubs of many different shapes and sizes, suitable for every garden, large or small.

Corylus maxima 'Purpurea'

Corylus maxima 'Purpurea' is grown for its large, heart-shaped leaves that are a rich dark purple in colour. It produces purple tinged catkins in winter and edible nuts that ripen in autumn.

Height and spread:	5 x 5m (16 x 16ft)
Cultivation requirements:	Fertile, well-drained soil in full sun
Place of origin:	Garden origin
Suitable for:	Purple leaved shrubs make the ideal foil for plants with yellow, orange or dark red flowers, or grasses and shrubs with golden foliage. *C. maxima* 'Purpurea' is a large shrub and is best at the back of a border

Fatsia japonica

Fatsia japonica is an evergreen shrub notable for its large, glossy, lobed leaves and creamy white umbels of flowers that are followed by spherical, black fruit.

Height and spread:	1.5 x 4m (5 x 13ft)
Flower colour:	Creamy white
Cultivation requirements:	Fertile, moist but well drained soil in full sun or semi shade. In very cold climates a sheltered courtyard or cool conservatory or greenhouse may be needed
Flowering time:	Autumn
Place of origin:	South Korea and Japan
Suitable for:	*F. japonica* is an excellent architectural plant, particularly effective against hard landscaping such as stone and rock. It is also suitable as an under-storey plant at a woodland edge

Ilex aquifolium 'Pyramidalis Aureomarginata'

Ilex aquifolium 'Pyramidalis Aureomarginata' is a highly decorative, upright form of the common holly, with gold margined leaves and red berries. Hollies are dioecious – plants are either male or female, so both must be grown if berries are required – and this cultivar is female, so male hollies will be needed nearby to ensure cross pollination.

Height and spread: 6 x 5m (20 x 16ft)
Cultivation requirements: Moderately fertile, moist but well drained soil in full sun
Place of origin: Garden origin
Suitable for: Variegated evergreen shrubs make a pleasant addition to the winter garden and provide year round presence. Grow in a mixed border or as a specimen

Mahonia japonica 'Bealei'

Mahonia japonica 'Bealei' is an erect, evergreen shrub with blue-green, pinnate leaves and bright yellow flowers. It has strong architectural presence, making it the ideal foil for modern materials such as steel and aluminium or hard landscaping of rock and stone. It is equally at home in a mixed border, as part of a woodland planting or in a winter garden, where its winter flowers and strong foliage will make quite an impact.

Height and spread: 2 x 3m (6 x 10ft)
Flower colour: Yellow
Cultivation requirements: Moderately fertile, moist but well drained soil in full sun or partial shade
Flowering time: Winter
Place of origin: Garden origin
Suitable for: Early colour in a mixed border, as an alternative to a hedge it can be used as an informal screen planting

Perennials

Perennials are, broadly speaking, plants that have a life span of more than one year, coming into leaf and entering their reproductive cycle (flowering) after a period of dormancy, which is usually but not always during winter. Many perennials die back to ground level during their dormant period, but others are evergreen. Technically, trees and shrubs are also classed as perennial, as they too fill most of the above criteria. However, for the purpose of practical gardening the term perennial does not include woody plants.

There are literally tens of thousands of perennials suitable for the garden, with everything from low growing ground plants such as *Heuchera* 'Firefly' to massive border plants like *Helianthus salicifolius*. Perennials often provide the main floral element in the garden during spring and summer and their spent flowers and seed heads can also provide interest well into the depths of winter.

An effective planting scheme with year round interest will often include a good proportion of perennials. The great joy of gardening with these plants is that, whilst many are long flowering 'solid performers', others are brief but spectacular shooting stars, providing endless variation and anticipation to the flower garden.

Gaura lindhiemeri

Gaura lindhiemeri is a superb perennial noted for its long flowering season. It has wiry stems and small, well spaced leaves, so from summer into autumn the overwhelming impression is of its flowers which are small, four petalled and irregularly star shaped.

Height and spread:	Up to 1.5m x 90cm (5 x 3ft)
Flower colour:	White or pale pink
Cultivation requirements:	Moist but well drained soil in full sun or light shade. *G. lindhiemeri* is largely drought tolerant
Flowering time:	Summer to mid-late autumn
Place of origin:	USA, Texas and Louisiana
Suitable for:	A mixed border, herbaceous border, naturalistic planting and low irrigation gravel garden. Because of its loose, lax habit, *G. lindhiemeri* is excellent growing through more upright plants or shrubs that have light foliage and are sparsely furnished with branches near the base

Salvia nemorosa 'Lubecca'

Salvia nemorosa 'Lubecca' is a compact plant, suitable for the front of a border, that produces beautiful violet flowers with reddish purple bracts. The blooms are highly attractive to invertebrates, especially bees and moths.

Height and spread:	45 x 45cm (18 x 18in)
Flower colour:	Violet/purple
Cultivation requirements:	Moist but well drained soil, not too rich in nutrients, in full sun or light shade.
Flowering time:	Summer to mid-autumn.
Place of origin:	Garden origin
Suitable for:	A mixed border, herbaceous border and low irrigation gravel garden. This plant associates well with low growing grasses such as *Nasella trichotoma* and bulbous plants including *Eremurus* 'Cleopatra'.

Hemerocallis 'Golden Chimes'

Hemerocallis 'Golden Chimes' is one of the best of the golden flowered day-lilies, a group of plants with so many cultivars that the choice can be bewildering at times. An evergreen perennial, it has deep golden yellow flowers that are an attractive reddish brown on the reverse and is a particularly free flowering plant.

Height and spread:	90 x 90cm (35 x 35in)
Flower colour:	Yellow
Cultivation requirements:	Fertile, moist but well drained soil in full sun. Flowering time: summer
Place of origin:	Garden origin
Suitable for:	A mixed border or herbaceous border. *H.* 'Golden Chimes' forms good clumps making it suitable for ground cover

Nepeta 'Six Hills Giant'

Nepeta 'Six Hills Giant' has strongly aromatic flowers and foliage. Its leaves are grey/green and hairy and it produces its lavender-blue flowers over a very long period, making it an invaluable garden plant and one that is well used by bees. It is one of a group of plants known as 'Catnip', owing to the intoxicating effects they have on felines! On hot, sunny days this plant exudes aromatic oils that are equally as attractive to humans.

Height and spread:	90 x 60cm (36 x 24in)
Flower colour:	Lavender blue
Cultivation requirements:	Well drained soil in full, drought tolerant
Flowering time:	Early summer to mid-autumn
Place of origin:	Garden origin
Suitable for:	A mixed border, herbaceous border, path edge, as ground cover with roses and for a low irrigation gravel garden

Geranium psilostemon

Geranium psilostemon is an excellent addition to any garden, having good strong foliage that colours well in autumn and gorgeous, dark-centred magenta flowers. If the old flowering stems are cut back near to the ground, it will often produce a second flush of flowers and plenty of fresh foliage.

Height and spread:	1m x 60cm (3 x 2ft)
Flower colour:	Magenta
Cultivation requirements:	Moist but well drained soil in full sun, fairly drought tolerant
Flowering time:	Summer
Place of origin:	Caucasus and Turkey
Suitable for:	A mixed border, also highly effective with shrub roses and ornamental grasses. Try *G. psilostemon* with the straw-coloured flower stems of *Calamagrostis* 'Karl Foerster' for a lovely contrast of colour and form

Eupatorium purpureum

Eupatorium purpureum is a big, strong perennial with plenty of presence for the back or middle of a border. It has a 'naturalistic' appearance that makes it suitable for wilder areas of the garden, but is equally at home in a more formal setting. Flowering for a fairly long period, it is attractive to many invertebrates.

Height and spread:	2.2 x 1m (7 x 3ft)
Flower colour:	Variable from white through pink to purple, most commonly the latter
Cultivation requirements:	Moist – but not wet – soil in full sun or partial shade
Flowering time:	Mid-summer to early autumn
Place of origin:	Eastern USA
Suitable for:	A mixed border, wild garden, or naturalistic planting

Verbena bonariensis

Verbena bonariensis has, justifiably, become a hugely popular plant in recent years. Its virtues are many: long flowering, versatile, excellent for wildlife including birds and invertebrates, and possessing the ability to lend a contemporary air to planting schemes. It is also highly tolerant of drought and will self seed without becoming invasive.

Height and spread:	1.8m x 45cm (6ft x 18in)
Flower colour:	Lilac purple
Cultivation requirements:	Free draining soil that is not too rich in nutrients, in full sun. Excessive feeding and watering will cause the plant to become overly tall at the expense of flowers
Flowering time:	Mid-summer to late autumn
Place of origin:	South America, Brazil to Argentina
Suitable for:	A mixed border, gravel garden, as a massed planting with grasses

Ornamental Grasses

Ornamental grasses have been around for a long time; Gertrude Jekyll was using them in planting schemes during the early part of the 20th century. Despite that, their true potential has only recently begun to be exploited, as for a long time grasses tended only to be used in association with other grasses.

The strengths of ornamental grasses are their long season of interest – up to 10 months of the year – their architectural and structural presence, foliage form and colour and the more subtle qualities such as the rustling sound they make as the wind passes through them.

Ornamental grasses vary from small, front of the border plants to large structural specimens. They are loosely grouped into cool season (early flowering) and warm season (late flowering) plants, giving a good spread of flowering interest from early summer through to late autumn.

Some grasses are evergreen but the majority are treated as herbaceous perennials, requiring cutting back in early spring. They associate very well with shrubs, flowering perennial and bulbous plants. Their architectural qualities lend themselves to contemporary plantings, and some of the world's leading garden designers utilize this fashionable group of plants extensively in modern designs, mixing them with other plants at will.

Stipa gigantea

Stipa gigantea is one of the finest of the large grasses. It is especially effective because of the see-through nature of its flowering stems, which create height without bulk. These stems are surmounted with beautiful panicles of golden, oat-like spikelets, the outer husks of which persist well into winter. Although a large plant, these qualities make it suitable for most gardens.

Height and spread:	2.5 x 1.2m (8 x 4ft)
Cultivation requirements:	Moderately fertile, well drained soil in full sun, *S. gigantea* is highly tolerant of drought.
Flowering time:	Mid-summer
Place of origin:	Spain and Portugal
Suitable for:	Mixed plantings, herbaceous borders, gravel gardens

Calamagrostis x acutiflora 'Karl Foerster'

Calamagrostis x *acutiflora* 'Karl Foerster' is an erect grass with tightly packed stems that make it highly suitable as a 'punctuation mark' in borders, or, when closely planted, as a background screen planting. Its pink-bronze inflorescences fade to a straw-like buff colour and persist well into winter.

Height and spread:	1.8m x 60cm (6 x 2ft)
Cultivation requirements:	Although preferring moist but well drained, humus rich soils, *C.* x *acutiflora* 'Karl Foerster' will tolerate poorer soils and drought. Full sun or partial shade.
Flowering time:	Mid-summer
Place of origin:	Garden origin
Suitable for:	Mixed borders, as an architectural specimen, gravel gardens

Elymus magellanicus

Elymus magellanicus is a compact grass that is grown for its stunning, steel-blue foliage. It has insignificant flowers, but this really does not matter – it is the foliage that really counts with this plant. It makes an excellent foil for other plants, in particular those with really hot orangey-red flowers such as the Californian fuchsia, *Zauscheneria californica*.

Height and spread:	30 x 30cm (12 x 12in)
Cultivation requirements:	Moist but well drained soil in full sun. Tolerant of drought
Place of origin:	Southern Chile and Argentina
Suitable for:	The front of a mixed border, path edge or a gravel garden

Miscanthus 'Ferne Osten'

Miscanthus 'Ferne Osten' is a member of a very large group of grasses, miscanthus. *M.* 'Ferne Osten' is one of the most compact, with beautiful autumn foliage tinted red and orange, and attractive, creamy flowerheads.

Height and spread:	80 x 50cm (31 x 20in)
Cultivation requirements:	Fertile, moist but well drained soil. Although tolerant of partial shade the best autumn colour is achieved in an open, sunny site
Flowering time:	Late summer into autumn
Place of origin:	Garden origin
Suitable for:	The front of a mixed border, path edge, or in a winter planting

Bulbous Plants

The term bulbous refers to plants that include true bulbs (daffodils, for example) but also plants that grow from tubers, corms and rhizomes. These are, in effect, storage organs that enable bulbous plants to cope with difficult growing conditions and long periods of dormancy, during which time there is often nothing or little of the plant visible above ground.

Because many bulbous plants tend to be adapted to tough environments, this makes them invaluable in a garden setting. Many are suitable for the kind of thin, dry and nutrient deficient soil found at the foot of a hot and sunny wall. Others can cope with dry shade and are therefore ideal for planting under deciduous or even evergreen trees, where nutrients and soil moisture are at a premium. There is a wide range of bulbous plants that are suitable for naturalizing in grass and consequently it is possible to create a 'floral carpet' in turf over a long period, from winter flowering crocuses right through to early summer flowering Camassia.

Bulbous plants are also good in a mixed border, where they provide colour without occupying much space, given that they have usually died back when most perennials are in active growth. Other bulbous plants such as Agapanthus and Canna are later flowering and very showy, making them perfect for the mixed summer border or, in the case of canna, sub-tropical plantings.

Agapanthus caulescens

Agapanthus caulescens (the new name for *Agapanthus* Headbourne Hybrids) is a clump forming plant with narrow, strap like leaves that broaden near the top of the plant. It bears open umbels of bell shaped flowers from summer to autumn.

Height and spread:	1m x 60cm (3 x 2ft)
Flower colour:	Violet-blue
Cultivation requirements:	Moist but well drained soil in full sun. *A. caulescens* is not completely frost hardy and will require over-wintering in colder climates
Flowering time:	Mid-summer to autumn
Place of origin:	Swaziland
Suitable for:	Ideal for growing in a container, where the restricted root run will encourage flowering, or in a border in warmer climates. Agapanthus have become invasive in parts of Australia, and should not be grown where there is a threat to native flora

Canna 'President'

Canna 'President' is an upright rhizomatous perennial grown for its foliage effect as much as its flowers. The leaves are large, blue-green and glossy and make a effective foil for the racemes of flowers.

Height and spread:	1.2m x 50cm (4ft x 22in)
Flower colour:	Scarlet
Cultivation requirements:	Fertile soil in full sun, ideally in a sheltered site. Cannas require plenty of water during dry periods
Flowering time:	Mid-summer to early autumn
Place of origin:	Garden origin
Suitable for:	A mixed border, foliage border or sub-tropical planting. Cannas are not hardy in colder climates and should be lifted and stored in late autumn

Iris reticulata

Iris reticulata is a bulbous, low growing winter flowering iris. The blooms are fragrant and variable in colour, having a yellow central ridge on each fall. This is a good plant to grow at the base of a sunny wall, where the soil is dry and well drained, and the plant protected by the rain shadow of the house.

Height and spread:	10–15cm x 5cm (4–6in x 2in)
Flower colour:	Variable from pale to deep blue through to purple
Cultivation requirements:	Well drained soil, ideally neutral to slightly alkaline, in full sun. Drought tolerant but not suitable for areas where winter rainfall is high. Suitable for growing in an alpine glasshouse. After flowering the bulbs of *Iris reticulata* sometimes split and if this happens it can be some years before they reach flowering size again
Flowering time:	Winter to early spring
Place of origin:	Caucasus, Turkey
Suitable for:	A rock garden, alpine trough or alpine house

Narcissus 'Minnow'

Narcissus 'Minnow' is a dwarf daffodil producing pale yellow flowers which appear in mid-spring. It spreads rapidly but is not particularly invasive, although this tendency to spread can be at the expense of its flowers. However, because *Narcissus* 'Minnow' does spread and is fairly robust, it is one of the daffodils that are most suitable for naturalizing in a lawn, where it will withstand a degree of wear and tear, and compete well with the grass. Plant bulbs into the turf with a bulb planter in patterns or simply a random clump.

Height:	18cm (7in)
Flower colour:	Pale yellow cups with cream perianth segments
Cultivation requirements:	Fertile, well drained soil that retains some moisture during the growing season. Full sun or dappled shade
Flowering time:	Mid-spring
Place of origin:	Garden origin
Suitable for:	The edge of a border or in light shade around the bases of deciduous trees

Annual Plants

Annual plants are those that complete their lifecycle within one growing season, that is, they germinate from seed, grow to flowering size, flower and set seed. Ornamental annuals are invaluable garden plants, as they can provide a riot of colour for a limited cost, and can help to 'fill gaps' in borders. Some annuals are self perpetuating in that they will set seed and germinate in situ each year. Others may need to be reintroduced each year, either as plug or pot plants, or by direct sowing outdoors into prepared ground.

Nigella damascena Persian Jewel Series

The Persian Jewel Series are a mixed colour cultivar range of *N. damascena*. The colours range from deep blue to violet, rose pink to white. The foliage is finely divided and almost fern like.

Height and spread:	50 x 20cm (20 x 8in)
Flower colour:	Variable
Cultivation requirements:	Well drained soil in full sun. *N. damascena* is drought tolerant and can be direct sown in spring
Flowering time:	Summer, or until late autumn with successive sowing
Place of origin:	Southern Europe and North Africa
Suitable for:	A gravel garden or sunny border

Lobelia erinus 'Crystal Palace'

Lobelia erinus 'Crystal Palace' is actually a perennial, but one which is more usually treated as an annual because it will not over-winter in colder climates. Compact in form, it has tiny foliage and an abundance of flowers.

Height and spread:	10 x 10cm (4 x 4in)
Flower colour:	Dark blue
Cultivation requirements:	Reliable moist, fertile soil in full sun. *L. erinus* 'Crystal Palace' can be over-wintered if given a deep, dry mulch of straw, but is best treated as an annual and replaced each year
Flowering time:	Summer to autumn
Place of origin:	Garden origin
Suitable for:	Trailing over a low wall or as an edging for a container. Can also be used as a border edging plant

Eschscholzia californica

Eschscholzia californica is a fabulous annual poppy with sunny, mostly orange flowers and delicate grey-green foliage. It produces long, narrow seed pods which split open with an audible crack.

Height and spread:	30 x 15cm (12 x 6in)
Flower colour:	Variable
Cultivation requirements:	Free draining, gritty soil in full sun. *E. californica* will germinate when sown in situ
Flowering time:	Summer
Place of origin:	California, south-east North America
Suitable for:	A gravel garden, rock garden or the edges of a gravel path. Can be used in a border if the soil is not too rich

Biennial Plants

Biennial plants are those that take two seasons (or years) to complete their life cycle. In the first year they develop from seed to produce foliage; during the second year they develop flowers, then fruit and set seed.

By sowing seed of biennial plants in successive seasons it is possible to have a continuous display of flowers, and the plants themselves will, in many cases, set seed too, adding to the succession. Biennials are useful in a garden, as they tend to seed around into unexpected places, often where it would be very difficult to plant anything, and so they lend a naturalistic look.

Digitalis purpurea Excelsior Hybrids

Digitalis purpurea Excelsior Hybrids are cultivated hybrid forms of the common foxglove, bearing flowers in pastel shades of purple, pink, soft yellow and white. The flowers are arranged horizontally around the flower spike and open from the bottom of the spike upwards in turn.

Height and spread:	1–2m x 60cm (3–6ft x 24in)
Flower colour:	Variable
Cultivation requirements:	Tolerant of a range of soils except very dry or very wet. Ideally grow in humus rich soil in full sun or light shade
Flowering time:	Early summer
Place of origin:	Garden origin
Suitable for:	A wild garden, naturalistic planting, a woodland garden or else in a mixed border

Myosotis sylvatica 'Blue Ball'

Myosotis sylvatica 'Blue Ball' is a short lived perennial or biennial, usually treated as the latter. It has the classic, yellow eyed, blue forget-me-not flowers and hairy, grey-green leaves. It will often self seed around in a garden, but is not invasive and can easily be removed.

Height and spread:	12–30 x 15cm (5–12 x 6in)
Flower colour:	Blue
Cultivation requirements:	Moderately fertile moist but well drained soil, in full sun or partial shade
Flowering time:	Spring to early summer
Place of origin:	Garden origin
Suitable for:	Bedding schemes, the edge of a mixed border or wildflower border

Lunaria annua

Lunaria annua is a biennial or annual, grown for its attractive flowers but also for its flat, rounded, translucent seed pods that the botanical name notes – lunaria as in 'moon-like'. This plant should be allowed to seed around so that it can 'pop up' through other plants in a natural, unplanned manner.

Height and spread:	90 x 30cm (36 x 12in)
Flower colour:	Variable, white to light purple
Cultivation requirements:	Fertile, moist but well drained soil, in full sun or partial shade
Flowering time:	Late spring and summer
Place of origin:	Europe
Suitable for:	A wild garden or mixed border

Climbers

Climbers add a vertical dimension to the garden that is especially useful in smaller spaces. They also excel at 'hiding' ugly features such as fences, can be trained over attractive features like pergolas or arches, or can stand alone, trained onto an obelisk or a simple 'wigwam' of canes or posts. Some climbers are useful for extending the season of interest by allowing them to grow through other plants. For example, an old apple tree can become a living support for a climbing rose, or an early flowering shrub can be combined with an easily controlled climber like *Eccremocarpus scaber*. Combining different climbers – roses and clematis being a classic combination – ensures a long season of interest. Choosing climbers that flower at different times will offer the longest display, but combining plants with flowering seasons that overlap with each other often provides the greater interest.

Climbing plants use a variety of methods to cling on and climb. Some have twining leaf stalks that wind around supports or other plants; others have aerial roots that can burrow into brick and mortar; others still have tendrils, adhesive pads or thorns to help haul themselves upwards. Because of this, care needs to be taken when selecting climbing plants as some – ivy

Vitis coignetiae

Vitis coignetiae is an ornamental vine that supports itself by tendrils. It is grown for its large, heart-shaped leaves that colour spectacularly in autumn with red, yellow and bronze tints. Although it produces small, blue-black grapes, they are only of ornamental value, as they are unpalatable.

Height:	15m (49ft)
Cultivation requirements:	Well drained, humus rich soil in full sun or partial shade – the best autumn colour is achieved when the plant is in full sun
Place of origin:	Korea and Japan
Suitable for:	Growing up a wall, on trellis or through a large, robust shrub that will not be swamped by this vigorous vine

being the classic case – can cause damage to mortar on buildings.

Fixing tensioned wire on vine eyes or erecting trellis on tile battens will prevent damage to mortared walls.

Hedera helix 'Atropurpurea'

Hedera helix 'Atropurpurea' is a form of common ivy with large, five lobed dark green leaves. During periods of cold weather, the leaves turn a rich bronze-purple, the mid-ribs and veins remaining green. It uses aerial roots to climb and provide support.

Height:	8m (26ft)
Cultivation requirements:	Ivies are pretty tough plants – although some of the variegated forms are more tender – and once established can tolerate a range of conditions including deep shade and dry, nutrient poor soil. However, they establish best in humus rich, alkaline soil that is moist but well drained
Place of origin:	Garden origin
Suitable for:	Can be grown against a wall – if mortar damage is not an issue – otherwise, against trellis. Although ivies are often grown through trees, this is only suitable if their growth can be controlled; they should not be allowed to get up into the crown of the tree

Passiflora caerulea

Passiflora caerulea is a fast growing hardy passion flower that climbs by using twining leaf stalks. It has bowl shaped white or pink tinged flowers with blue and white zoned centres. These are followed by ovoid yellow fruit that are edible but rather tasteless.

Height: 10m (33ft)
Flower colour: White to pink with blue and white coronas
Cultivation requirements: Moist but well drained soil, ideally in full sun or partial shade and with shelter from drying winds
Flowering time: Summer to autumn
Place of origin: Central and Western South America
Suitable for: Growing on wires or trellis against a wall, on a free standing obelisk or through a robust shrub

Ipomea tricolor 'Heavenly Blue'

Ipomea tricolor 'Heavenly Blue' is a fast growing annual climber with twining stems. It has attractive, heart shaped leaves and beautiful, funnel shaped bright blue flowers. As an annual this is one of the climbing plants best suited to growing through others, as it will not impede their growth or damage them in any way.

Height: 3–4m (10–13ft)
Flower colour: Blue, occasionally purple
Cultivation requirements: Moderately fertile, well drained soil in full sun.
Flowering time: Summer to autumn
Place of origin: Garden origin
Suitable for: Growing through other climbers or shrubs or on free standing plant supports

Aquatics

A water feature is always an attractive proposition, as it brings sound and movement to the garden as well as being the single most important feature to have if you hope to attract wildlife into your garden. However, water is also tricky to manage as the balance between healthy, clean water and a soupy green mess can be hard to strike.

Aquatic plants have a key part to play in ensuring that ponds and lakes remain healthy, and there are a wide range of plants suitable for different circumstances. A balanced planting for a pond will include marginal plants, those that occupy the fringes of the pond with their roots in the water and foliage and flowers above, deep water plants that remain submerged or that send up foliage and flowers to the surface of the water – like water lilies – oxygenating plants that can simply be dropped into the water, and floating plants that float on the surface without setting down roots.

Alien invaders

Great care should be taken when purchasing aquatic plants to ensure that they are not invasive, as in recent years there has been an increase in 'escaped' alien plants becoming a serious nuisance in waterways, and threatening to destroy natural habitats and kill off native aquatic plants. Aquatic plants are easily spread, and even if you think your pond is isolated from other bodies of water, remember that waterfowl landing on your pond will carry seed and parts of plants to other bodies of water. Ask your supplier for advice before purchasing any aquatic plants, and take care to thoroughly wash new plants in clean water before planting to reduce the risk of introducing seeds or pieces of plants that are invasive.

Nymphaea 'Perry's Pink'

Nymphaea 'Perry's Pink' is a free flowering water lily with cupped, pink flowers and rounded leaves. Suitable for a pond of any size this is one of many bred by the prolific water lily breeder Perry Slocum.

Flower colour:	Pink
Cultivation requirements:	Neutral to mildly acidic water, full sun
Flowering time:	Mid-summer to autumn
Place of origin:	Garden origin
Suitable for:	Any pond providing it has a depth of at least 1m (3ft)

Pontederia cordata

Pontederia cordata is a marginal aquatic plant that will grow in up to 20cm (8in) deep of water. It has attractive, lance shaped leaves that are held above the water and floating on it. These are followed by spikes of attractive blue flowers.

Height and spread:	1.2m x 75cm (4ft x 30in)
Flower colour:	Blue
Cultivation requirements:	Plant in a loam filled planting basket at a depth of not more than 20cm (8in), in full sun
Flowering time:	Late summer
Place of origin:	North America
Suitable for:	A sunny position in a pond

Nuphar lutea

Nuphar lutea is a deep water aquatic perennial with floating, ovate to rounded wavy margined leaves that are reminiscent of water lily leaves. It produces yellow flowers in summer with a rather unpleasant smell.

Spread:	2m (7ft)
Flower colour:	Yellow
Cultivation requirements:	Plant in acid water around 30–40cm (12–16in) deep. As *N. lutea* requires a free root run it is not suitable for planting in an aquatic basket, but instead the roots should be weighted down into the mud at the bottom of the pond
Flowering time:	Summer
Place of origin:	Eurasia, N. Africa, West Indies, E. USA
Suitable for:	Ponds with a surface area less than 60 sq m (66 sq yd). Note: *Nuphea advena* is an American cousin of *N. lutea*, but instead of a 2m (7ft) spread *N. advena* spreads indefinitely. It is NOT recommended for planting in ornamental ponds

Myriophyllum verticillatum

Myriophyllum verticillatum is an oxygenating plant with attractive, bright green leaves that are comb-like as they emerge above the water line. In summer a yellow flower spike is also held above the water line.

Spread:	Indefinite. An indefinite spread is common for oxygenating plants, however this does mean that great care should be taken to ensure that the plants you choose are native to your country (see 'Alien invaders', page 41). *M. verticillatum* will require regular trimming back
Flower colour:	Yellow
Cultivation requirements:	Grow in an aquatic planting basket filled with loamy soil
Flowering time:	Summer
Place of origin:	Europe, Asia, N. America
Suitable for:	Any pond, providing it does not connect with external waterways

Stratiotes aloides

Stratiotes aloides is a floating aquatic plant with rosettes of prickly, saw-toothed leaves. These rosettes surface at flowering time, when cup shaped white or off pink flowers are produced. After flowering the rosettes drop back below the water surface, where the deeper water does not freeze.

Spread:	Indefinite, must be kept in check
Flower colour:	White, occasionally off pink
Cultivation requirements:	Alkaline water over 30cm (12in) deep, full sun
Flowering time:	Summer
Place of origin:	Europe, Asia
Suitable for:	A sunny pond. This is a vigorous plant that will take over if not regularly reduced. Plants that are removed should be composted and not allowed to reach open waterways

Roses

Roses are among the most beautiful of all flowering plants, and as a consequence have been a favourite for hybridization and breeding programmes for well over a century. Roses are usually divided into two major groups, Old Garden roses and Modern roses, which are then further subdivided into numerous sections – almost 30 in all. These complex subdivisions, added to the general, though often misplaced belief that roses are excessively prone to pest and diseases, lead many gardeners to conclude that roses are specialist plants to be avoided.

Although it is true that some of the older roses can fall prey to pests and diseases more easily than other plants, it is actually the way in which we use roses that hinders their chances of success. Rather than planting them in monoculture, roses should be treated as any other flowering shrub and mixed with perennials, annuals and shrubs. In this way the risk of pests and diseases is dramatically reduced, as the roses form part of a mixed planting where there is a natural succession of flowering and form, and where natural predators are more likely to be able to control any pest problems.

As well as beautiful flowers, many roses also boast attractive fruits (hips) and foliage. Some of the older roses, including the species roses, are remarkably tough plants which are perfectly capable of withstanding poor soil and drought.

Rosa glauca

Rosa glauca is a species rose notable for its very attractive foliage, quite unlike that of any other rose. The leaves are bluish-grey, dusky pink beneath, divided into five to nine leaflets that are narrowly elliptic. The cerise pink flowers are followed by attractive brown hips that ripen to red.

Height and spread:	2 x 1.5m (7 x 5ft)
Flower colour:	Pink
Cultivation requirements:	This is a robust plant that is capable of withstanding exposed conditions and drought, as well as poor soils. Richer, moister soil will encourage a bigger plant. Full sun
Flowering time:	Summer
Place of origin:	Mountainous regions of central and southern Europe
Suitable for:	A mixed border, foliage garden, gravel garden. *R. glauca* associates superbly with ornamental grasses

Rosa 'Alexander'

Rosa 'Alexander' is a large flowered bush rose (formerly known as Hybrid Tea roses) with shiny, dark green foliage and a vigorous, upright habit. These particular characteristics lend themselves to a formal, controlled planting.

Height and spread:	2m x 80cm (7ft x 31in)
Flower colour:	Bright red
Cultivation requirements:	Moist but well drained, humus rich soil in full sun. Large flowered bush roses perform best on heavier soils and grow less well on light sandy soil
Flowering time:	Summer to autumn
Place of origin:	Garden origin
Suitable for:	Mixed borders

Rosa 'Complicata'

Rosa 'Complicata' is a gorgeous Gallica rose (roses that are usually of a dense free branching habit, thorny stems and single or double, usually fragrant flowers) with strong arching growth. The leaves are greyish green, the flowers single, slightly cupped and fragrant.

Height and spread:	2.2 x 2.5m (7 x 8ft)
Flower colour:	Pink
Cultivation requirements:	Another tough and resilient rose that will tolerate poor soil and tough conditions but also grow well in better soils. Full sun
Flowering time:	Summer
Place of origin:	Garden origin
Suitable for:	A mixed border, gravel garden, associated with grasses and perennials

Rosa 'Hyde Hall'

Rosa 'Hyde Hall' is a vigorous English shrub rose with an arching habit and attractive foliage. Regular deadheading will ensure a long flowering period.

Height and spread:	1.8 x 1.5m (6 x 5ft)
Flower colour:	Dark pink
Cultivation requirements:	Moist but well drained, humus rich soil in full sun
Flowering time:	Summer to autumn
Place of origin:	Garden origin
Suitable for:	Any mixed border

Rosa 'Little White Pet'

Rosa 'Little White Pet' is a compact, free flowering polyantha rose (Polyantha roses are compact growing with few thorns, glossy leaves and sprays of flowers). Low growing, its sprays of double white flowers are red in bud, making a lovely contrast.

Height and spread:	45 x 55cm (18 x 22in)
Flower colour:	White
Cultivation requirements:	Moist but well drained, humus rich soil in full sun
Flowering time:	Summer to autumn
Place of origin:	Garden origin
Suitable for:	The front of a mixed border, cascading over the front of a wall or as a path edging

Rosa 'Breath of Life'

Rosa 'Breath of Life' is an upright climbing rose with beautiful apricot double flowers that are fragrant.

Height and spread:	2.5 x 2.2m (8 x 7ft)
Flower colour:	Apricot to apricot pink
Cultivation requirements:	Moist but well drained, humus rich soil in full sun
Flowering time:	Summer to autumn
Place of origin:	Garden origin
Suitable for: A	fence or trellis, growing through a shrub, or on a plant support such as an obelisk

Alpines

Alpine plants are among the most interesting and, on occasion, challenging plants to grow. As a result they are often viewed as specialized plants solely for the enthusiast, and it is true to say that many alpines plants do require that degree of expertise and dedication, and specialist equipment for that matter.

However, there are many alpines that are easy to grow and tough too, making them excellent plants for containers and troughs, raised beds and gravel gardens and for planting into walls or amongst paving slabs.

Because of their compact size it is possible to have a large selection of alpines in a comparatively small space, making them ideal for small gardens, patios and balconies, and those gardeners who want to garden and collect plants without lots of heavy, manual work.

Anchusa cespitosa

Anchusa cespitosa is a delightful little plant with rosettes of narrow, dark green leaves. These linear, hairy leaves can grow up to 6cm (2⅜in) long. In the centre of each rosette, clusters of flowers of the most vivid blue form are produced, each with a white eye. These delicate flowers are only 1.2cm (½in) across. *Anchusa cespitosa* is a dwarf species of the Anchusa genus, which are all found in dry, stony or rocky sites.

Height and spread:	10 x 15cm (4 x 6in)
Flower colour:	Blue
Cultivation requirements:	Sharply drained soil in full sun. Will not tolerate waterlogging
Flowering time:	Spring
Place of origin:	Mountainous regions of Greece
Suitable for:	The edge of a path in a gravel garden, planted in a sunny wall or rock bank, alpine trough

Pulsatilla vulgaris

Pulsatilla vulgaris is one of the most beautiful of all spring flowers. It is perfectly adapted to the difficult habitat in which it is found in the wild – limestone rock outcrops with little soil. With leaves and stems densely covered by silvery hairs and gorgeous flowers, this is a plant that is well worth finding a little space for.

Height and spread:	15 x 20cm (6 x 8in)
Flower colour:	From deep to pale purple
Cultivation requirements:	Fertile but very well drained alkaline soil. *P. vulgaris* will often migrate – seeding into a part of the garden where conditions are more favourable
Flowering time:	Spring
Place of origin:	Northern Europe to the Ukraine
Suitable for:	A rock garden, alpine trough, gravel garden

Gentiana 'Multiflora'

Gentiana 'Multiflora' is an evergreen, low growing perennial with trailing stems and glossy dark green leaves and stunning, trumpet shaped deep violet blue flowers.

Height and spread:	10 x 25cm (4 x 10in)
Flower colour:	Deep violet blue
Cultivation requirements:	Humus rich, acid soil that is light and well drained but reliably moist. Full sun or partial shade
Flowering time:	Spring
Place of origin:	Mountainous regions of central southern Europe
Suitable for:	A rock garden, alpine trough, gravel garden

Cacti & Succulents

Cacti and succulents are a group of plants in which there has been growing interest in recent years. Whilst many are not fully hardy in colder climates, increasing experimentation in this area and, of course, the fact that many of these plants are suitable for growing in containers or for 'bedding out' in the summer months means that the opportunities for using cacti and succulents in gardens are growing all the time and the plants are consequently becoming more popular.

Cacti and succulents are among the most self-sufficient of all plants. In the wild they usually grow in quite extreme conditions – desert cacti, for example, might have to cope with searing day time heat and freezing sub-zero temperatures at night – but the one thing they all resent is very wet conditions. Consequently, good drainage is the key to the successful cultivation of cacti and succulents. Whilst some plants in this group are quite tiny, others are magnificent architectural plants.

Agave americana

Agave americana is a strongly architectural monocarpic succulent. It has rosettes of large, fleshy, sword shaped leaves that are armed with spikes.

Height and spread:	2 x 3m (7 x 10ft)
Flower colour:	Yellow–green. *A. americana* will grow for many years before flowering, whereupon it dies
Cultivation requirements:	Very well drained soil in full sun
Flowering time:	Summer
Place of origin:	Mexico
Suitable for:	A gravel garden, as an architectural specimen in a container

Opuntia robusta

Opuntia robusta is a shrubby or tree like cactus with thick, flat oval leaves that are grey-green or blue and tipped with white spines. It has bowl shaped yellow flowers followed by deep red fruit.

Height and spread:	2 x 2m (7 x 7ft)
Flower colour:	Yellow
Cultivation requirements:	Sharply drained, moderately fertile soil in full sun
Flowering time:	Late spring/summer
Place of origin:	Central Mexico
Suitable for:	A desert or gravel garden, in a container or a temperate greenhouse

Sempervivum 'Reinhard'

Sempervivum 'Reinhard' is a mat forming succulent with emerald green rosettes of leaves that are tipped with contrasting black. It bears reddish pink flowers on thick, leafy stems during summer.

Height and spread:	8 x 30cm (3 x 12in)
Flower colour:	Red/pink
Cultivation requirements:	Well drained gritty soil in full sun
Flowering time:	Summer
Place of origin:	Garden origin
Suitable for:	Ideal for crevices in a rock garden, alpine troughs or pans

Ferns

Ferns are among the most ancient of plants alive on the planet today, and their survival is a testament to their adaptation to the environments in which they grow. Ferns are superb foliage plants, many are tolerant of dry shade, others preferring damper conditions.

As a group, ferns associate well with spring bulbs – when the fronds of the ferns are beginning to appear – but especially with lush foliage plants such as Hosta and Darmera. They are also very effective with ornamental grasses, particularly Deschampsia, or in large drifts on their own. Some ferns are epiphytic (growing on other plants but not parasitic), others terrestrial, some seemingly interchangeable!

Despite their ancient heritage, ferns can be used in highly contemporary planting schemes and are very effective with modern materials and stone.

Polystichum setiferum

Polystichum setiferum is an attractive fern with dark green, spreading fronds arranged in shuttlecocks. *P. setiferum* 'Herrenhausen' is a compact form, particularly suitable for a shady container.

Height and spread:	1.4m x 90cm (5ft x 36in)
Cultivation requirements:	Fertile soil that is humus rich but well drained in either partial or full shade
Place of origin:	Europe
Suitable for:	A massed planting in a shady corner, a woodland under story

Dryopteris

Dryopteris is a large genus of terrestrial ferns from mainly temperate regions in the northern hemisphere. Mostly deciduous, they are found on stream sides, in woodland and among rocky crags. *D. erythrosora* is a stunning fern with young fronds coloured bronze – red when young, eventually turning green. Usually deciduous, it can remain evergreen in mild winters or in a sheltered site.

Height and spread:	60 x 40cm (24–16in)
Cultivation requirements:	Humus rich soil that is reliably moist. Partial shade, or full sun with shade at midday.
Place of origin:	China, Japan.
Suitable for:	A mixed shady border with grasses and sedges, moist woodland.

Dicksonia antartica

Dicksonia antartica is a tree fern that has become very popular in recent years. The 'trunk' is actually an erect rhizome covered in roots, from the top of which the fronds emerge, pale green at first but then darkening.

Height and spread:	up to 5 x 4m (16 x 13ft)
Cultivation requirements:	Humus rich acid soil in partial to full shade, although they will tolerate full sun with a plentiful supply of water to the rhizomes
Place of origin:	E. Australia, Tasmania
Suitable for:	A woodland glade, a modern container, as an architectural feature plant

Orchids

Orchids must rank amongst the most evocative of all cultivated plants. Wild terrestrial orchids create a sense of excitement that almost no other plant can – and in the case of some species can lead to exhaustive measures to protect them from over zealous and ill advised collectors. The location of the last remaining colony of slipper orchid in the UK, for example, is a closely guarded secret known only to a few people. Terrestrial hardy orchids have a complex symbiotic relationship with the soil and the fungal mychorriza therein, making their cultivation problematical. They should never be collected from the wild without the full approval of the relevant authorities, although some can be purchased from reputable growers who have cultivated them in nursery conditions.

The 'house plant' type of orchids can be epiphytic, lithophytic (meaning growing among or on rocks and stones) or terrestrial, and they engender a similar reaction of awe. The extraordinary beauty of their flowers has attracted interest for well over a century, and prompted many intrepid individuals to go in pursuit of new species in some of the most challenging parts of the world. Once collected and introduced, their cultivation was often viewed as being steeped in mystery and complexity.

In more recent times, however, it has been plant breeders rather than plant collectors who have made the biggest contribution to the range of orchids available. They have created a vast array of hybridized plants with seemingly endless variations of flower size and colour.

Cultivated epiphytic orchids make excellent house or conservatory plants. Many will benefit from a change of environment during the course of the year – moving from a warmer room to a cool room and a shady spot outdoors in summer, for example. However, extremes of temperature should be avoided.

Cymbidium

Cymbidium are a genus of terrestrial, epiphytic and lithophytic evergreen orchids from tropical and temperate regions. Plant breeders have produced literally hundreds of winter and spring flowering cultivars. *C.* 'Showgirl' is a terrestrial orchid with long, narrow leaves. The flowers are borne in upright racemes and are pale pink with red mottling and stripes on the lips.

Height and spread:	40 x 40cm (16 x 16in)
Cultivation requirements:	Cymbidiums are cool growing orchids requiring bright but filtered or indirect light in summer and good ventilation. Watering moderately, an orchid feed should be applied every third watering or via a dripper, with misting carried out at least once a day. During winter months the plant should be placed in full light and only watered occasionally
Flowering time:	Winter to spring
Place of origin:	Hybrid
Suitable for:	A cool conservatory/glasshouse or as a houseplant

Indoor Plants

Indoor plants can bring a sterile environment to life and introduce a calming influence, as is borne out by studies showing how office workers perceive an improvement in their work place when plants are introduced. As most indoor plants are evergreen, it is their foliage effect that is most highly regarded, although some indoor plants also have the benefit of attractive flowers. There are also 'cross-over' plants – those that can be grown outdoors and indoors such as azaleas and cyclamen. It is important to note, though, that many of these plants have been bred for a short but spectacular display indoors, and do not always cope with the outdoor environment.

There are a range of indoor plants suitable for most conditions – bright sunlight and warm to cool and shady –

although as a general rule direct sunlight should be avoided. In our modern, centrally-heated (and air-conditioned) homes the greatest threat to indoor plants is the risk of drying out, so regular misting, at least twice a day, is highly recommended.

It should also be remembered that indoor plants all have outdoor homes in the wild, so regular feeding and re-potting are important. When re-potting it is not essential to go up a pot size each time – you could soon end up with some very large indoor plants! – but it is important to replace a reasonable amount of compost. Indoor plants in peat- or coir-based composts can dry out and become difficult to re-wet. In this case, fill a watering can or jug and add a few drops of washing up liquid to the water, before irrigating the plant. The washing up liquid helps the water molecules to 'bind' themselves to the compost.

Dracaena marginata 'Tricolor'

Dracaena marginata 'Tricolor' is one of the most tolerant and robust of indoor plants, making it easy to grow. It has straight stems topped with a cluster of arching, linear leaves that are striped cream, pink and green. Plants with multiple stems are the most decorative.

Height and spread:	3 x 1.5m (10 x 5ft), but can be controlled by pot size
Cultivation requirements:	Ideally, a loam based indoor plant compost with a controlled release fertilizer incorporated
Place of origin:	Cultivar

Bonsai

The art of bonsai is over 1,000 years old, and distinct from almost every other facet of horticulture. Bonsai (the closest literal translation is 'tray planting') involves the manipulation of plants to create idealized forms in miniature, according to pre-defined codes. For example, popular forms of bonsai include formal upright, a single tree with a straight stem and root over rock, where the young roots of the tree are pegged down over a rock and into the planting tray.

Plants are further manipulated by recreating the effect of lightning strikes and dead wood 'stags' heads', by using small power tools to strip away bark and cambium. The main method of growth restriction comes through annual root pruning, where the plant is taken out of its planting tray, the compost removed and between one quarter and a third of the roots are pruned back before replanting with fresh compost. Leaf size is restricted by pinching out some or all of the first flush of leaves, causing a second flush of leaves to appear that are much diminished in size (see also page 84).

Ficus retusa Bonsai

Serissa foetida Bonsai

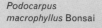

Podocarpus macrophyllus Bonsai

Although many bonsai specimens are highly prized and extremely valuable – indeed some are so old as to be priceless – there is nothing to stop the budding enthusiast from experimenting. If you are starting out, it is best to work with tree seedlings, which are cheap to buy or grow from seed and readily available. Studying the work of bonsai artists will give you an idea of what can be achieved, although the skill involved is considerable – but well worth the challenge!

Plant Adaptations

The most successful gardens are those that have been planted with suitable plants. It sounds obvious, but the old adage of 'the right plant in the right place' is occasionally overlooked. Sometimes, this is due to a lack of research – understanding the conditions in the garden and taking the appropriate action – and sometimes it is due to a strong desire to grow a particular group of plants that simply will not survive in the prevailing conditions. So if your garden is dry with thin, chalky soil, then trying to grow rhododendrons, for example, is likely to be a challenge not worth taking on.

Fortunately, there are hundreds of plants for every type of garden – sun or shade, exposed or sheltered, wet or dry – and for every type of soil. Many of these plants will tolerate a range of conditions, but some have become highly specialized. So, just as a desert fox has large, thin ears to help regulate body temperature in extreme conditions of heat, plants such as lavender, for example, are physiologically adapted to their home environment; in this case the dry, hot hillsides and scrub around the Mediterranean and Asia.

Understanding and recognizing these adaptations will enable you to choose the right plants for your garden, in so doing saving time and money and avoiding the frustration of seeing healthy plants dying, simply because they are the wrong plant in the wrong place. After a while, you will find spotting the right plants for your garden becomes quite easy – intuitive really – which will help you to fight off the temptation to buy attractively packaged plants that are cleverly presented for sale at the garden centre. These kinds of impulse buys should be avoided if at all possible, as they can often end in costly and frustrating failure.

Plant Adaptations for Hot, Dry Conditions

Often considered the hardest conditions in which to garden, drought and heat are actually suitable for a broad range of plants that cope admirably on the leanest of diets. If you have a particularly hot, sunny garden, with well drained or poor soil, look out for plants with the following physiological adaptations which make them especially suitable for such tough conditions:

Small leaves help to reduce water loss – transpiration – which is especially important in exposed locations where the wind can

Always choose plants which are suited to the prevailing conditions

Agave americana originally comes from the desert, so it is perfectly adapted to hot, dry conditions

Retreating below ground to avoid summer heat is an adaptation employed by many bulbous plants. In some instances the plants will emerge and flower in spring – such as tulips and alliums – whilst nerines and amaryllis flower in autumn.

Hairy leaves To trap any available moisture in the air some drought tolerant plants have conspicuously hairy leaves. Often these plants grow in very thin soil or straight out of rock, such as the British native *Pulsatilla*

Putting it all together

Whilst many plants have developed one or two specific adaptations to cope with tricky conditions, some plants take advantage of a whole range of adaptations. *Rhodiola rosea*, commonly known as Roseroot, is found in dry, rocky habitats throughout the northern hemisphere. In order to survive it has developed a number of adaptations:

- Thick, fleshy rhizomatous roots
- Low growing to 30cm (12in), so that the wind passes over it
- Silvery grey leaves
- Small leaves
- Succulent leaves

literally suck the life from plants. By reducing their surface area, the leaves of plants like *Rhodanthemum hosmariensis* transpire less, helping to keep the plant alive and healthy

Silver or grey leaves help to reflect sunlight and form one of the most easily distinguishable features of drought tolerant plants, so it is fair to say that if a plant has silver leaves it will cope with dry conditions. Many of these plants, such as *Artemisia arborescens*, are superb foliage plants.

vulgaris. In some cases the leaves are so hairy that they have the texture of fur and *Stachys byzantina* has gained the common name of 'Lamb's Ears' as a result.

Waxy leaves help to slow down transpiration and reduce leaf scorch in extremely hot weather. *Cistus populifolius* has very waxy leaves and attractive white flowers.

Thick, fleshy rosettes of leaves have an expanded cellular structure capable of holding moisture over a long period. *Agave americana* is a classic example, hailing from

Drought tolerant plants are often distinguished by silvery grey-green leaves, like this *Artemisia arborescens*

the extremely dry deserts of southern north America. Perhaps *Aloe vera* is the most widely known, although more for its cosmetic qualities.

Tap roots Long thick tap roots such as those of *Eryngium* x *oliverianum*, help to secure the plant in the ground, quest for moisture and store moisture and starch.

Low growth prevents excessive transpiration in windy conditions and reduces wind damage. The dwarf mountain pine, *Pinus mujo*, is low growing and has waxy leaves to reduce transpiration.

Spaced out stems Thin, widely spaced flowering stems allow wind to filter through the plant, reducing transpiration and preventing it from being torn from the ground. The beautiful golden oat grass, *Stipa gigantea*, is a perfect example.

The golden oat grass, *Stipa gigantea*, has perfectly adapted form for reducing transpiration

Plant Adaptations to Low Light Levels

Just as plants have developed strategies to cope with hot, dry and exposed conditions, so they have adapted to situations where light levels are low, such as temperate woodlands and forests. Here the competition is with two factors: other plants, especially established trees, and the conditions resulting from a dense canopy of plants. Underneath the tree canopy conditions can be dry – a consequence of the available soil water being drawn up by the trees – and shady, with limited light available for essential functions such as photosynthesis.

If your garden has a shady corner, go for plants with large, dark green leaves, whilst around deciduous trees and shrubs consider planting early-flowering bulbs. Plants with running roots can be useful in colonizing otherwise difficult areas, and by improving the soil as much as possible it is more likely that the roots will run. Plants are naturally drawn towards the light, and robust

Fatsia japonica is perfectly adapted to a life in shady conditions

Common ivy, *Hedera helix*, uses other plants as supports in order to climb towards the light

Phoenix from the flames

Some plants have remarkably clever strategies that rely on natural phenomena to procreate. The Wellingtonia, *Sequioadendron giganteum*, is a native of North West America, where it forms large forests of towering evergreen trees. In such an environment the soil beneath is dry and lacking in nutrients, with low light levels. Hardly ideal for the seedlings of Wellingtonia to establish, but the parent plant takes advantage of a primal force: fire! The Wellingtonia's seeds need the regular forest fires that occur during hot summers to break down a hard outer coating. The fire also clears scrubby vegetation and the resulting ash enriches the soil, making it ideal for the emerging seedlings. The parent plant cannot be harmed, as it has developed a remarkable bark that is thick and spongy and perfect for withstanding heat damage.

flowering climbers or foliage plants such as Vitis can be useful for livening up dark, weighty plants like Leyland cypress.

To combat these challenging growing conditions, plants have developed the following strategies:

Large leaves An excellent example of this are the leaves of the stunning *Rhododendron sinogrande*. By increasing the surface area of its leaves, as much light as possible is absorbed for photosynthesis for the plant.

Running, rhizomatous roots This particular characteristic enables plants, such as the beautiful woodlander *Anemone hupehensis*, to 'relocate' by spreading out towards areas where conditions are more favourable. The common bramble and stinging nettle employ the same strategy.

Climbers The ability to climb towards the light, using other plants as a support. Many woodland plants do this, such as ivy (Hedera) and honeysuckle (Lonicera).

The extraordinary looking Swiss cheese plant, *Monstera deliciosa*, is another clever climber

and the light levels are therefore comparatively high. A number of quintessential woodland plants do just that – the English bluebell *Hyacinthoides non-scripta*, and the north American woodlander, *Trillium grandiflorum*, are both excellent examples of this particular type of plant.

Epiphytism This term simply means the ability to grow on a host plant without actually being parasitic and preventing its host from flourishing. Some of the ferns and many of the orchids can establish themselves high up in the woodland canopy, living on a host plant and yet drawing nutrients not from the host, but from the environment.

Dark pigmentation Many woodland plants have leaves with conspicuously dark pigmentation. Unlike the silver leaved plants of hot, dry and sunny locations, woodland plants need to absorb as much sunlight as possible in order to photosynthesize. The dark pigmentation is as a consequence of the concentration of chlorophyll, required to absorb the light available.

Another example is the popular indoor plant *Monstera deliciosa*, otherwise known as the Swiss cheese plant, which combines an ability to reach along the forest floor and clamber up the trees of its native rainforests, with the distinctive large leaves that makes this plant such a household favourite for growing indoors.

Early flowering By completing flowering and setting seed early in the season, many woodland floor plants take advantage of the fact that the majority of trees have not yet come into leaf,

Trillium grandiflorum is an American woodland plant that flowers early in the season to take advantage of higher light levels

Tools & Equipment

To garden successfully you need a range of suitable, basic tools. The main battery of tools in the gardener's armoury are hand tools, many of which have remained unchanged in design for centuries. This could be, and often is, proof that a good design cannot be improved upon, but in the case of digging tools – forks and spades – an interesting anomaly arises. These tools were developed primarily for mining and quarrying, where workers used them mainly in the kneeling position. For some strange reason – perhaps miners and quarrymen gardened keenly in what little spare time they had – these tools became co-opted into the garden without any design change, making them horribly awkward and tiring to use for taller gardeners. Fortunately, there are companies that manufacture long-handled tools, albeit at the specialized end of the market.

Although tool handle lengths have remained largely untouched by the passage of progress, there have, over the years, been a whole litany of weird and wonderful inventions designed to make gardening easier, from the sublime to the ridiculous. It has to be said that few of these inventions have stood the test of time, simply because the 'original' basic tools are better than the mad cap alternatives.

Before purchasing any tools, it is worth considering how much use they are likely to get and what features you have in your garden that require specific tools to maintain them. For example, a bigger garden usually equals more use, as does heavier soil, in which case you might want to invest in heavier-duty, more expensive tools. And obviously there is no need for hedging shears if you do not have a hedge.

Digging & General Tools

The two most frequently used and perhaps most versatile tools for gardening are the humble spade and fork – although they are actually not so humble, as there are a number of variations on the theme.

Border fork – a small fork with a narrow head, designed for working in and around plants.

Digging fork – a larger fork designed for (can you guess?) digging!

Muck or dung fork – larger head than the digging fork, with curving, slender tines. Used for shifting dung and turning compost.

Hay fork – larger still, although similar in appearance to the dung fork. In the right hands a hay fork can be used to lift a very large amount of hay or any plant material.

Border spade – a small-headed spade for working around plants.

Digging spade – designed very much for digging, robust and with a larger head. Some have foot plates welded to the top of the blade to make digging more comfortable.

Ditching/trenching spade – a narrow head tapering to a vee for ditching, digging post holes and so on. Although the domestic gardener is unlikely to embark on large scale ditch digging, this spade is useful for digging post holes as its narrow head means it can reach a greater depth.

Shovels – there are a wide range of shovels available, from the classic builder's shovel through to large headed, lightweight models for shifting mulch or snow.

Hand digging tools

These are, in effect, baby versions of the tools above, designed for close work in small areas or specialized jobs such as bulb planting. The main hand digging tools are:

• trowel
• hand fork
• specialized bulb planters

To which can be added a range of more obscure items designed for removing weeds from lawns, for example. A good hand trowel and fork and one bulb planter are usually more than adequate.

Left to right: a muck or dung fork, a digging fork and a border spade

Left to right: hand bulb planter, long-handled planter, thin-headed trowel, flatter-headed trowel and hand fork

Tools for weeding

This has been one of the main areas for strange inventions, perhaps because weeding is something that every gardener does, with varying degrees of enthusiasm. Obviously weeding can be carried out by hand pulling, or by using a fork or hand fork, but the specifically designed tool is the hoe. Again, there are variations on the theme, the draw hoe having a blade at 90-degrees to the handle and used by pulling back across the soil, whilst the Dutch hoe has a blade that comes straight from the handle and is utilized with a stabbing motion, cutting weeds off at the base.

Shears

There are three main types of shears, two designed primarily for use on grass, the other more versatile and suitable for a variety of tasks. The two grass shears are:

Border shear – with long handles and blades that lie flat to the soil (rather like long-handled hedge shears).

Edging shear – with upright blades for cutting crisp edges around borders.

Hedge shears – these have short handles and are designed primarily for trimming grass.

Left to right: long-handled edging shears, spring tine rake, short-handled hedge shears and a landscape rake

Choosing materials

The type of tools you choose to buy will depend on several factors, including the amount of money you can spend, the type of garden you have and the amount of work required. Bear in mind these considerations when weighing up the pros and cons of buying tools made from different materials.

- **Wooden handles** may seem old fashioned, but they are durable and have a degree of natural flex. They do need regular maintenance however, including annual sanding down and the application of linseed oil ideally twice a year.
- **Plastic handles** require no maintenance and have a degree of flex, but can perish if left outdoors for long periods. They eventually become brittle and prone to breaking.
- **Metal handles** are durable and require little or no maintenance, but they add significantly to the overall weight of the tool and can be unpleasant to use in very cold weather.
- **Stainless steel** is the ideal material for the tool head, being durable and requiring no maintenance. The downside is the cost, which is usually twice as much as non-stainless.

The performance of shears depends mainly on the quality of their blades, so it is worth investing in as good a quality blade as you can afford. With long-handled shears check that there is not too much flexing in the handles, which can be a nuisance.

Rakes

There are two main types of rake, the first being used primarily for soil cultivation, the second for leaf raking, scarifying grass and so on:

Landscape rake – this has a flat head, rather like a hair comb, made from metal or wood.

Spring tine rake – the latter type of rake can come in a variety of forms, but the most popular is the spring tine rake, with flexible tines fanning out from the base of the handle. These tines are usually made from light gauge metal; there are also plastic variants, but these tend to be less well suited to the rigours of grass scarifying.

Power Tools

Power tools can help to make gardening easier by speeding up many of the jobs which, traditionally, would have been carried out using hand tools. The most common power tool used by gardeners is probably the lawn mower, but hedge trimmers, brush cutters and rotary cultivators are also widely used. The two main sources of power for power tools are electricity and petrol/diesel, and there are advantages and disadvantages to both.

Powered hedge trimmers

Hedge cutting is undoubtedly made much easier by using powered hedge trimmers. These use a reciprocating blade (sometimes two blades) mounted over a fixed bar to achieve the cut. Powered hedge trimmers either have one long, single-sided blade or, more commonly, two shorter two-sided blades. The advantage of the former is their longer reach, usually at the expense of increased weight, whilst two-sided blade machines can cut in a 'back and forth motion' and tend to be more compact and lighter in weight.

Brush cutters

Brush cutters – also known as strimmers – are, in effect, the modern successor to the scythe. A revolving head, which spins at high speed and is mounted with either a metal blade or nylon lines, is fitted to a drive shaft connected directly to the engine.

Brush cutters are useful for cutting rough grass and brush, the sort of longer vegetation that a mower would struggle to cope with.

Rotary cultivators

Unless you have a particularly large garden, you are unlikely to want to buy a rotary cultivator, but for cultivating large areas of soil they can be very useful and are usually available for hire. Rotary cultivators have rotating tines that turn over the soil, with a backboard and depth control that can be adjusted to vary the depth of cultivation and the quality of the tilth.

Lawn mowers

Lawn mowers can be divided into two categories, based on the method by which they cut.

Rotary mowers – These type of mowers have a single, centrally mounted blade fitted to a nut beneath the cutting deck (thereby forming two cutting edges). The rotating action of the blade helps to pull the grass upright as the mower passes over. Rotary mowers are either mounted on four wheels or with two wheels at the front and a driven roller at the rear. Grass clippings are

A rotary cultivator is an invaluable tool if you regularly need to turn over soil, but most gardeners will usually hire rather than buy such a piece of equipment

Electric power or petrol/diesel

Electrically powered machines have a number of advantages; they are usually lighter than petrol/diesel machines, much quieter and pleasant to operate as they do not produce fumes. However, they rely on a supply of electricity, and consequently their reach is dictated by the proximity of the power supply and length of cable. Petrol or diesel machines are usually more powerful than their electric counterparts and more versatile, as there is no need for them to be tethered to a power supply.

collected in a box (or more often a soft bag) attached to the rear of the machine.

Rotary mowers are more versatile than cylinder mowers, because:

• they can cut grass regardless of whether it is long or short, high or low quality
• they are simpler to build, so consequently cheaper to buy
• on-going maintenance is easier

The quality of cut, however, is never as high as that from a cylinder machine.

Cylinder mowers –These have several blades (five to seven being the norm for most mowers of this type) arranged around a central axle, forming a cylinder. In front of this cylinder a metal 'comb' helps to flick up the grass into the path of the blades. Because of this the quality of cut tends to be very high, as the length and frequency of blade contact with the grass is great. As cylinder mowers are almost always driven by a rear mounted roller, they produce the classic striped effect on the grass, because the roller lays the grass in the direction of travel. Grass clippings are collected in a 'box' mounted in front of the cylinder.

The main disadvantages of cylinder mowers are that:
• they are unsuitable for longer grass or grass varieties that produce tough flowering stalks, as the cylinder tends to pass over these without removing them,

leaving an unsatisfactory finish
• they are more complex and costly to build, so more expensive to buy
• on-going maintenance costs are higher

However, if you are growing a high-quality grass mix and are aiming to achieve a bowling green-style lawn, then the cylinder mower cannot be beaten.

Hover mowers These are a type of rotary mower without wheels or rollers which move by gliding on a cushion of air, making them easy to handle and ideal for smaller gardens and sloping sites, but unsuitable for creating a striped effect to the lawn. Most are powered by electricity, but petrol versions are available which can be used on larger lawns. They are also easy to store as they are light enough to be hung up. One major drawback, however, is that most are not designed to collect grass clippings – an extra chore to consider! Also, it is normally not possible to alter the height of the cut.

A cylinder mower is the best option for a high quality, very flat lawn, but these models lack versatility

Gardening gloves – essential for tough jobs or when working with prickly plants.

Eye and ear protection – make sure these items conform to relevant safety standards.

Garden line – for marking out border edges and positioning plants.

Garden twine – for tying in climbing plants; a biodegradable twine is ideal.

Watering equipment – including hoses, hose reels, watering cans and so on.

Sprayers – for misting indoor plants and applying pesticides or organic compounds.

Any active gardener needs a whole range of different aids and accessories in order to be properly equipped

Roller or wheels?

Pedestrian lawn mowers are either mounted on four wheels, or two wheels plus a roller (rotary mowers), or just a roller (cylinder mowers). In the case of self-propelled pedestrian mowers it is usually either the rear wheels or the cylinder that drive the machine.

Rollers create a striped effect on the grass and enable the mower to cut right up to the edge of a flower bed without dropping over and scalping the grass. The disadvantage of roller driven mowers is that they are unsuitable for long or wet grass. Wheel only mowers are better for longer, wetter grass, but will not stripe the lawn and can cause scalping on the edges of borders.

Accessories

As well as the essential hand tools and suitable power tools, a range of accessories will help the gardener with a number of common gardening tasks, including:

Wheelbarrow – essential for moving mulch, compost and so on. There are many different types on the market.

Safety first!

All power tools have risks associated with their use. Apart from injury caused by the operation of the tool – the blades of a hedge trimmer for example – there are also injury risks from fuel, risk of electrocution and so on. Follow these steps for safe and trouble free operation of power tools:

- Always read the safety advice that will come with the tool, and never make adaptations to the tool that could compromise safety features or lead to a dangerous malfunction.
- Wear the appropriate safety gear and clothing – eye protection, ear defenders, gloves and close fitting clothes that will not get caught in the moving parts of a machine.
- Make sure your power tools are serviced regularly and stored correctly.
- Always take care when refuelling petrol or diesel machines; refuel in the shade and never leave fuel cans in direct sunlight where combustible vapours can form.
- When using electric power tools, either use a low voltage adaptor or a circuit breaker to avoid electrocution.
- Keep the cable of electric tools away from cutting parts. This can be done by passing the cable through the handle of a digging fork securely driven into the ground, a couple of metres (yards) or so away from where you are working.
- Always check the area you are about to work in before commencing. Look out for objects that may damage the machine or get flicked up dangerously, particularly by brush cutters or mowers.

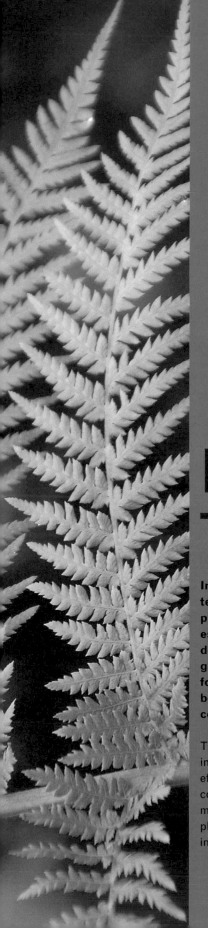

Planting Techniques

In this chapter we will look at the different planting techniques that apply to a variety of plants. Correct planting is essential to ensure the successful establishment of plants, and there are a number of different techniques that can be employed by the gardener to ensure this. The correct spacing of plants for maximum impact and the diverse effects that can be achieved through the combination of plants is also covered in this chapter.

Tips are given on plant combinations and associations, including how to combine colour, shape and form to the best effect, including contrasting foliage shapes and flower colour. Furthermore, the correct spacing of plants for maximum effect is also dealt with, a crucial aspect of planting if borders are not to become overcrowded and individual plants overwhelmed.

Buying Trees & Shrubs

Trees and shrubs are offered for sale in a variety of ways. How you choose to buy will depend on the effect you want to achieve, your budget, and how patient you are!

Tree Size

A key consideration when buying a tree is what size to opt for.

Seedling (or transplant) The smallest a tree can be purchased, these are cheap to buy but take a while to establish. Some gardeners grow them on in containers for a couple of years before planting out.

Whip One or two years old, and named because they tend to have a single clear stem with no side branches, whips combine reasonable size with value for money.

Feathered maiden Over two years old and with a number of good side branches. Good for planting in quantity or establishing on sites where conditions are tough.

Light standard A recognizable tree, with a clear trunk (unless multi-stemmed) topped with a substantial crown. Combines impact with reasonably good value for money.

Thereafter, tree sizes increase as follows: standard, heavy standard, extra heavy standard and so on, right up to mature trees.

Buy big or small?

It may seem tempting to buy as large a tree as possible, but there are a number of potential problems if you do so. A tree may suffer from being transplanted; there may be root damage from lifting; and a large tree will require daily watering during the growing season, for perhaps as long as three years. As a general rule, smaller trees establish far more quickly than larger ones when transplanted, as the root damage is minimal and the plant can establish with comparative ease. Indeed, a tree planted as a whip can often outstrip the same species planted at the same time but as a standard – and for a fraction of the price and aftercare costs.

Root System

Trees are also sold according to how their root systems have been grown and then packaged for sale:

Bare root These are trees that are field grown and then lifted and bagged on order for despatch. This is common for trees offered at smaller sizes – whips and maidens – but not usual in a garden centre where stock has to have a long shelf life. There are a number of advantages to this:

- bare root plants are only available during their dormant period, so you are certain to be planting them at the correct time
- the roots make immediate contact with the soil in the garden so usually establish more rapidly and grow more healthily
- pots and potting compost cost money and add to haulage costs, so bare root plants tend to be cheaper as well

Bare root plants are generally cheaper and will establish more quickly than ones that are pot-grown

Specialist nurseries offer a wide selection of trees in different sizes

Be careful not to damage the root ball when handling a root balled plant

Root balled These trees tend to be larger and will have been 'undercut' for two or more seasons, which creates a smaller root system comprised mainly of fibrous roots. When the tree is lifted it is immediately placed in a burlap or Hessian sack and bound with wire mesh. Do not remove this when the tree is planted, as it is designed to hold the root ball together and prevent damage to the delicate feeder roots.

Pot grown and potted Pot grown trees have spent their entire lives in pots. Potted trees are plants that have been field grown, then lifted and potted on for sale. Both pot grown and potted plants are also referred to as containerized plants.

Most plants are nowadays sold as potted specimens. The problem with plants in containers is that the composts they are grown in tend to be rich, moisture retentive and organic based, which is fine if your soil is a really good loam, but less helpful if you garden on heavy soils, especially clay. On clay soils the light compost can create a sump, causing water to settle around the plant roots and encourage rotting.

Re-potting into a loam based compost may help, alternatively make sure when planting that the planting hole is thoroughly forked over and the soil mixed with the correct ratio of compost (see below) to even out the differences.

Pot grown trees are convenient as they are easy to handle and transport

TIP

Containerized plants left too long in their pots will often become root bound. This is easy to spot: lift the plant from its pot; if the roots fill most of the pot space, it is root bound. In this instance, gently tease out some of the fine feeder roots from the root ball, which will help to encourage the plant to root into the surrounding soil.

Using Shrubs

Shrubs are usually purchased as container grown or containerized specimens in a wide range of sizes up to 20 litres (5 gallons) and more. As with trees, there are distinct advantages to planting smaller specimens.

Think carefully about what you want to achieve with the shrubs in your garden. Do you want them merely as a backdrop to other plants, or are there flowering shrubs that you want to bring to the fore? And what about using evergreen and winter flowering shrubs? All of these plants have a valuable role to play in your garden; where, how and whether you use them is for you to decide.

Shrubs can be planted singly as specimens, in groups of single species or mixed species, or in association with other plants – trees, perennials, bulbs and so on. Shrubs bring structure and solidity to the garden, and by selecting a range of shrubs with differing seasonal interest it is possible to have a broad diversity of colour.

Shrubs for colour

Foliage foil Some shrubs, such as the purple leaved *Cotinus coggyria* 'Royal Purple' or the golden *Viburnum opulus* 'Aurea' make a perfect foliage foil for other shrubs or perennials.
Colour combinations Combining purple and gold or silver and blue can make for a stunning combination. However, be careful when mixing variegated plants, and in particular avoid grouping plants that have gold variegation with those with white or silver variegation – the results can look decidedly uncomfortable.
Winter colour Shrubs that are grown for winter stem colour interest, such as *Cornus alba* 'Sibirica', *Salix* 'Britzensis' or *Rubus cockburnianus*, are best grown in groups of at least three plants, to maximize the effectiveness of the stem colour.

Planting Trees & Shrubs

Whatever size of tree you choose to plant, make sure you have checked the ultimate height and spread of the tree – trees can often grow surprisingly quickly – and have chosen a suitable location. Drive a stake into the ground to give an idea how the tree will look, then step back and contemplate to make sure you are happy with it.

Measure a square around the base of the pot or root ball that is at least half as big again all round [1]. A square hole has been shown to aid root establishment and penetration into the surrounding soil. If you are planting into grass, remove a thin layer of turf to the shape of the planting hole.

Start digging the hole, placing topsoil in one pile and subsoil in another. When you have reached the right depth – just a little deeper than the depth of the compost in the pot or the root ball, or in the case of bare root plants, at the nursery mark – dig over the base and sides of the hole with a fork, to aid root penetration.

Mix compost into the topsoil and subsoil removed from the hole, using about half as much compost as the total volume of soil. It is essential that this is really well mixed in. If you have removed turf in order to plant your tree, place this into the bottom of the hole with the turf side (green side) down.

Place the tree into the hole and at this point check the positioning again to ensure that the tree is presented as you want it. Begin backfilling the hole [2], alternating between subsoil and topsoil and firming with your heel as you go. If you are planting a bare root tree with a horizontal stake, hold the stake in position and fill as normal. Once filled, tie the tree to the stake with a tree tie [3]. Alternatively, if you are planting a root balled or containerized tree, when the hole is half filled, drive a stake into the ground at 45 degrees to the soil level so that the top half meets the trunk of the tree about 1m (3ft) up its length [4].

1

2

3

4

TIP

On heavy soils try mound planting your plants, an old technique that helps to keep plant roots out of the wet, preventing rots and aiding establishment. Dig a conventional planting hole, half as deep as the root ball of the plant, then create a topsoil/compost mound of around 30–40cm (12–16in) high over the hole. Plant into this, making sure to firm the soil well as you backfill.

The planting techniques for shrubs are just the same as when planting trees, although there is no need to use a stake for anything but the largest of specimens.

Watering in

As soon as you have finished planting, it is vital to water in the tree and continue watering regularly until established. Watering in is essential to settle the soil

Firm in newly planted trees and shrubs with the heel of your boot

around the roots as well as providing water that the plant can take up readily.

You will need to continue watering regularly during the first growing season.

Dam planting In particularly dry conditions create a dam around large, newly planted specimens by banking soil up to form a wall of around 30cm (12 in) high and 1m (3ft) diameter. When you water this dam will create a reservoir, helping to stop the plant wilting.

Wetting agent Adding a wetting agent of expanding crystals will cut down on watering.

Planting do's and don'ts – for trees, shrubs and perennials

Whatever you are planting there are a few definite dos and don'ts. Follow these rules and your plantings should establish quickly and successfully:

- **Don't** remove your topsoil from the planting hole and replace it with compost or imported topsoil, unless you are creating planting pockets in rock or pure gravel. However bad you may think your soil is, eventually the plants you plant will need to acclimatize to it, so mix one quarter to one third of compost with three quarters to two thirds topsoil.
- **Do** make sure that you make a planting hole that is plenty big enough for the root ball of the plant – ideally half again as big, and the same depth as the root ball. Loosen the soil in the base of the hole and at the sides.
- **Do** make sure the root ball of the new plant is evenly moist. It is often a good idea to stand the plant pots in water overnight (a pond being ideal for this). Remove the plant from its pot to check that the compost is well wetted.
- **Don't** make the hole too deep. When the plant has been placed in the hole the 'neck' of the plant – the point at which the green part of the plant emerges from the compost – should be above the surrounding soil level. Bare root plants will have an obvious mark (known as the nursery mark) where the soil level was before the tree was lifted. Planting too deeply creates the perfect conditions for lethal rots. On wet, heavy soil consider mound planting (see tip box, page 65).
- **Do** mix gravel or grit into the base of the planting hole – unless you are on very fast draining soil. This will aid drainage and reduce the risk of water-logging.
- **Don't** plant without first removing any weeds from the top of the compost. These seemingly innocuous weeds can become a major pest, growing out of the centre of the plant and often proving impossible to successfully remove.
- **Do** firm the soil around the plant as you backfill around the root ball. Use your hands or, in the case of larger plants, your heel. Good soil to root ball contact is essential if the new plant is not to dry out.
- **Do** water the plant in thoroughly, and continue to irrigate as required – usually once a week, but more during hot periods.

Planting Perennials

In many gardens perennials provide the most colour during the summer months, and many are also excellent structural foliage plants.

Perennials always look best when planted in quantity. There is a risk when using many single specimens of creating a bitty, 'dolly mixture' effect that can look too busy and unplanned.

Perennials for Colour and Height

One of the great pioneers of colour usage was Gertrude Jekyll, an English gardener who trained as an artist. She positioned plants in blocks or drifts, carefully balancing one colour against the next to achieve a natural, flowing effect. In a Jekyll scheme, the outer edges of a bed might start with a predominance of blue, giving way to purple, then lavender, oranges, yellows and reds.

In a smaller garden it can be difficult to plant single species in quantity, in which case try matching colours to create a similar effect to massed planting. For example, use five or six different plants that all have blue flowers, such as *Anchusa* 'Loddon Royalist', *Geranium* 'Johnson's Blue', *Agapanthus* 'Windlebrooke', *Ceratostigma plumbaginoides* and *Nigella damascena*. Although these plants will not all flower at the same time, you will maintain an even effect throughout the season.

A traditional way to plant borders is to follow a hierarchical scheme, where low growing plants occupy the front of the bed, medium height plants the centre and tall at the back, resulting in a tiered effect. While it is not a good idea to plant a big, solid plant at the front of a bed which obscures the rest of the planting, it is possible to be more creative with plant heights. A tall, translucent plant such as *Stipa gigantea* can create an interesting variation in a planting scheme.

Combining perennial plants in borders ensures both good colour and form in the garden

TIP

Blue is a recessive colour, and can seem more distant than it actually is; red, on the other hand, appears close even when actually quite distant. A short, wide garden will seem longer and squarer by using blue at the end and red at the sides, whilst a very long garden can be foreshortened with the use of red plants at the far boundary.

Ornamental grasses

Ornamental grasses should be planted in much the same way as perennials. They tend not to need fertilizers, although some of the Japanese grasses including Miscanthus and Imperata (Japanese blood grass, below) do prefer slightly richer, moister soils.

Buying and Planting

Perennials can be bought in a variety of sizes, from 9cm (4in) pot size up to 5 litres (10 pints) or more. I would always advocate planting smaller size plants as, generally, smaller plants establish more easily and need less watering. One exception would be when a real bargain arises: a keenly priced large perennial can be taken from its pot and split into several, smaller plants, making it good value for money.

Before planting, check the eventual size of the plant and make sure you are allowing enough space between it and the next plant in the border. Carefully slide the plant from its pot, aiming to avoid disturbance to the root ball [1]. Plant at once so that the roots do not dry out in a hole slightly wider than the root ball, and the same depth as the compost. Fill in around the plant so that the root ball is in close contact with the soil and there are no air pockets. Firm in well with your fingers [2].

1

2

Container plants have the advantage of being portable, so that colour can be instantly transferred

Supports

Many perennials require some form of staking or support if they are not to flop over under the weight of their foliage and flowers. The best time to stake perennials is before they

Some form of support not only helps a plant to establish itself but also directs the ultimate growth

have really got into active growth, usually in early to mid-spring. There are a number of different techniques that can be employed; using natural materials such as birch twigs to create a 'tepee' that can support the plant, making a 'basket' of willow or hazel stems, joined together with twine and then placed upside down over the crown of the plant, or using off-the-shelf plant supports that are made from metal or plastic and are driven into the soil around each plant.

Whatever materials are used, the most important aspect is to get the supports in early enough that plants grow through them rather than having to tie plants up later on, which results in an unnatural 'trussed-up' appearance.

Planting Bulbs

Bulbous plants can be planted in a number of different ways: as part of a mixed border, naturalized in grass, in containers, or amongst deciduous trees.

Bulbs in containers

Spring and autumn bulbs are excellent for extending the season of interest of planted containers. The best varieties to use are

those with a compact growth habit, unless the container is exceptionally large and capable of taking taller forms. *Crocus* 'Gypsy Girl' and *Narcissus* 'Tete a Tete' are excellent container subjects.

Bulbs in borders

When planting bulbs in borders, consider the effect you hope to achieve and the flowering time of the specimens you are planting. Early flowering bulbs such as Narcissus, tulips and crocus are best planted in clumps in a border, where they can provide a real splash of colour. However, later flowering plants that come into flower when most other perennial plants are also flowering, such as Eremurus and Allium, are better drifted through other plants where they will provide colourful highlights. The advantage of planting bulbs in borders is that their dying foliage, which can be rather unattractive, is obscured by the foliage of the other plants in the border.

Naturalizing bulbs in grass

The more vigorous crocuses such as *Crocus tommasinianus*, *C. nudiflorus* and *C. pulchellus* are suitable for naturalizing in grass, as are the species daffodils *Narcissus cyclamineus* and *N. bulbocodium* and compact narcissus cultivars such as *N.* 'Hawera'.

Scarifying When naturalizing bulbs in grass it is a good idea to scarify the lawn first with a rake or motorized auto-rake. This will help to reduce the vigour of the grasses,

but most importantly it will remove the thatch – the layer of dead grass at the root zone – which can impede water penetration to the bulbs and make planting more difficult.

Broadcast planting For maximum impact plant the bulbs in quantity, arranging them in big drifts. This is best achieved by broadcasting them – literally taking handfuls and casting them over the grass – and planting them where they fall, which will achieve a less contrived look.

New lawn If you are laying a new lawn from turf, you can plant the bulbs first and then lay the turf over the top. Once the bulbs have died down, usually by mid-summer, the area can be mown and the resulting material removed for composting.

Bulbs in a woodland setting

As many bulbs originate from the kind of dappled shade found at woodland edges or in glades, they are well suited to this kind of environment in a garden setting. Be sure to enrich the soil with leaf mould or garden compost before planting, as shady areas are usually nutrient poor. Plant bulbs such as snowdrops (Galanthus) and Erythronium in drifts between other shade lovers such as Heuchera, Tiarella and Epimedium.

Daffodils (Narcissus) are one of the best bulbs for naturalizing in large numbers across grassy areas and in lawns

TIP
- Plant spring flowering bulbs in autumn, and autumn flowering bulbs in spring.
- As a general rule, all true bulbs should be planted at a depth equal to two and a half to three times the length of the bulb, but always check the specific variety. Plants in the same 'bulbous group' as Cyclamen require different treatment, as the corm should be planted with its top level with the surrounding soil.
- When planting in heavy soil, add a handful of grit into the base of each planting hole to aid drainage and prevent rotting.

Planting Climbers

Before planting climbers, first consider the method of climbing support you can provide for them – will it be a fence or wall, an obelisk or pergola, and can you fit wires to the support to help train the plant along? Also, are you hoping simply to obscure an unattractive feature, or do you want the climber to become a focal point in its own right?

Using climbers in the garden

Obelisks and plant supports can be used to add structure and height to a border, even in relatively confined spaces.

Growing through shrubs Grow climbers through and over hedges and evergreen shrubs to add extra colour and interest; avoid really vigorous climbers as they might damage the 'host' plant.

Containers Annual climbers make excellent container plants, with a suitable support system such as birch twigs or hazel wands.

Screens and dividers Trained to freestanding trellis or a similar structure, climbers can be useful for dividing up a garden space, creating discreet areas. Sheds, bins and compost heaps can also be very effectively screened with trellis and climbers.

Step-by-step planting climbers against walls

Due to the rain shadow created by buildings, the soil at the foot of a wall is often dry and nutrient deficient. To overcome this, try the following:

TIP Think very carefully about the eventual size of the plants you are planting. The idea of a fast growing climber capable of hiding, for example, an unsightly building may seem attractive, but plants like the mile-a-minute vine (*Fallopia baldschuanica*) are not so called by accident, and can soon become a complete menace.

1

2

3

1 – Enrich the soil near, but not at, the base of the wall – about 50cm–1m (18in–3ft) away. Use plenty of well rotted organic matter. Remove the plant from its pot.

2 – Plant the climber in this prepared soil (50cm–1m/18in–3ft from the foot of the wall) and water it in well.

3 – Use trellis, bamboo canes or hazel/birch wands to create a support structure that will encourage the climber to grow up the wall. Mulch around the base of the climber using well rotted organic matter.

Training climbers

All climbing plants will perform better and be easier to manage and maintain if you have fitted the appropriate support system first. Fitting tensioned wires – wires that are pre-sprung and have had all of the slack removed from them – or trellis will reduce the risk of damage to walls by aerial roots or suckering pads.

The key to training climbing plants is to make sure you tie-in their extension growth regularly. Twine is commonly used to tie in climbers, and has the advantage of being biodegradable and having a degree of give.

Loop the twine around the support and tie it in, before forming a second loop with which to secure the stem

Planting Aquatics

Apart from floating aquatic plants, which extract the nutrients they need directly from the water, all aquatic plants require some form of growing media in which to root. In the case of natural, clay- and soil-lined ponds and lakes this is straightforward, as the plants will simply root into the fabric of the pond itself, in doing so often helping to stabilize it. But what if your pond has a plastic or butyl liner, or is made of concrete or fibreglass?

All aquatic plants except those that float need some sort of growing medium in which to establish properly

Here, there are two options. The first is to line the base and sides of the pond with a layer of soil, 10–20cm (4–8in) deep. Not only will this help with the natural rooting of many aquatic plants, it will also prove beneficial to pond organisms and invertebrates, which help to maintain a healthy balance and keep the water quality good. In this instance, bare rooted plants should be weighted with a large stone or brick, attached with plastic coated wire or twine, and then dropped into the water.

Planting aquatics in baskets

Aquatic plants can also be planted in special baskets, which are perforated at the sides to allow water penetration and root growth. These baskets are especially suited to plants like water lilies, deeper water aquatics that require a reasonable amount of soil to grow in. Follow these steps when planting in baskets:

Planting deep water aquatics

Deep water aquatics such as water lilies need to be gradually acclimatized to the depth of water in the pond. Water lilies throw up leaves to the depth of water they are in, and when purchased these leaves are usually on quite short stems. To start with, place the basket at a depth where the leaves are just below the surface level of the water. As the leaves break the surface, lower the basket again and repeat the process three or four times.

1 – Line the basket with hessian and fill it with a sterilized loam or clean topsoil – do not use fertilizers, which can adversely affect the quality of the water in the pond if they seep out of the basket.
2 – Place a top layer of gritty sand on top of the planting medium.
3 – Plant the aquatic into the basket, ensuring it is well firmed in.
4 – Dress the top of the basket with 5–10cm (2–4in) of pebbles or shingle to prevent the soil floating away into the pond.

Once the basket has been prepared and the plant is ready for the pond, gently lower the basket into the water. If the pond floor is uneven, consider using bricks or slabs to create a level base for the basket. Floating plants such as water soldier (*Stratiotes aloides*) can simply be thrown onto the water surface.

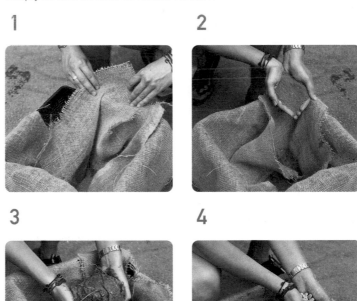

Planting Cacti and Succulents

Cacti and succulents can bring an interesting, exotic and architectural element to plantings. In frost-free, reliably warm areas the larger succulents (including the candelabra euphorbia) and cacti can be grown year round out of doors. In areas where winter frosts are prevalent, cacti are

Echeveria agavoides

best grown in containers that can be moved under cover in winter time, but there are a range of succulents that are quite hardy, such as the houseleek (Sempervivum).

Succulents also make excellent specimens when grown in 'pans':

Echinocactus grusonii is a good example of a cactus that makes a dramatic statement planted on its own

shallow pots, which are usually made from terracotta. By creating staged benching to display these pans, it is possible to create a superb setting for these usually small plants. Cacti, especially larger specimens, are very effective architectural plants and can be used to great effect as single specimens in modern planters, where they will create a sense of drama and excitement.

Planting in containers

Cacti and succulents require similar growing conditions of well drained, gritty soil and an open, sunny condition. In containers, use sterilized loam or a loam-based, low fertilizer compost mixed with plenty of grit [1]. Ensure good drainage from the base of the container by placing crocks (shards of broken pots) over the drainage hole. Gently press the succulents into the compost [2]. After planting, dress the top of the pot with more grit to prevent rot at the neck of the plant [3]. The end result is worthwhile [4].

Planting outdoors

Outdoors, improve the soil with plenty of sandy grit before planting. If you garden on heavy soil but want to use cacti and succulents, consider creating a raised rock garden where it may be possible to further manipulate the soil by removing the soil completely between rocks and replacing it with a light, gritty soil.

1

2

3

4

Planting Ferns

Ferns are grown as foliage plants, and are highly effective with other foliage plants that require similar growing conditions. So, the broad, thick leaves of hostas will contrast beautifully with the dissected fronds of *Dryopteris erythrosora*, and the long, leathery tongue shaped leaves of *Asplenium scolopendrium* are an effective foil for the feathery inflorescences of *Deschampsia cespitosa* 'Goldtau'.

Ferns can be used equally effectively on their own, and the sight of the emerging fronds of *Matteuccia struthiopteris* – so appropriately known as the shuttlecock fern – planted en masse, has a unique beauty.

Adiantum pedatum

Soil preparation for ferns

Although ferns can be grown in a variety of conditions from full sun to deep shade, in general they all prefer well prepared, humus rich but well drained soil. Incorporating plenty of organic matter, especially leaf mould or garden compost along with grit on heavier soils will help to create the right soil conditions. That said, ferns are actually pretty tough plants and in nature will often grow in the least promising of locations – in crevices in rocks or attached to the moss growing on a tree branch for example – but as is the case with all garden plants, they are a lot easier to manage and establish with a little soil preparation first.

Tree ferns

A glade of tree ferns (*Dicksonia antartica*) can make for an amazing, other-worldly sight given their prehistoric heritage, and as they are tolerant of sunny locations they also make very good subjects for containers. Just one or two tree ferns, mixed with other terrestrial ferns, can be equally effective.

Tree ferns do not have roots in the conventional sense (the fibrous 'trunk' is in essence the root system) and so irrigation to the 'trunk' by misting with water on a regular basis is very important, especially in dry, sunny conditions. They are also tender plants which are unlikely to survive outside of the mildest coastal and urban areas without some form of winter protection. Either grow in a pot and overwinter indoors, or protect the crown once the fronds have died back with a handful of straw tied in place with string.

As they are becoming increasingly threatened in some parts of their natural range, make sure that if you are buying a tree fern it comes from a renewable source.

Planting Alpines

Alpines are excellent plants to use if you are gardening in a small space or in a 'soil-less' garden, that is one that is entirely paved or concreted. This is because alpines can be grown in troughs, on rocks, in pans (shallow containers specifically designed for alpines) or under glass. The tougher, easier going alpines can be used as edging plants close to a path, or planted between paving flags in a patio. And of course they are very much at home in a rock garden, which can be anything from just a few rocks to a major feature.

How to grow alpines

Some alpines can be quite complicated to grow, some of them requiring a fair degree of experience and specialist equipment, and different cultivation requirements. However, in the simplest terms the cultivation of alpines can be described as follows:

- Alpines that can be grown outdoors all year round in temperate climates, given the right aspect and soil conditions, which can vary from full sun and well drained soil to shade and moist, peaty soil.
- Alpines that require winter protection with glasshouses, cloches or cold frames, mainly from excessive wet.

Creating an alpine feature

If you have an interest in alpines and are just starting out, try building up experience with the hardier types that can be grown outdoors all year round, perhaps by planting up an alpine trough or sink with a number of different species. This is a great way to grow alpines as the conditions – soil, aspect and so on – can be easily manipulated to suit the plants that you are growing, and aesthetically it is very pleasing, as you can really appreciate these often small plants in a setting that shows them to their best advantage.

Aubrieta is an indispensable plant for the rock or scree garden – one of the very best alpines

Sedum spectabile 'Brilliant' prefers slightly chalky, well drained soil

- Alpines requiring year-round protection under glass, usually in a cool but frost-free glasshouse.

Some alpines need well drained, gritty soil in full sun whilst others prefer well drained but humus rich soils. Check that you can accommodate the relevant cultural needs of plants.

Growing Indoor Plants

Of all the plants grown in and around our homes, indoor plants must be about the easiest to kill off! This is due to a number of factors relating to central heating and air conditioning – which create difficult growing conditions for plants as both dehumidify the atmosphere – and the fact that it does not rain indoors. Add to that the fact that many indoor plants stay in the same worn out compost for years on end and the recipe for disaster is complete.

Fortunately, many indoor plants on sale today have been selected for their ability to cope with degrees of neglect – indeed the aspidistra was commonly grown in the Victorian era as it was about the only plant capable of putting up with the pollution generated by gas lighting. But it does not have to be like this, as with regular attention and the occasional timely intervention it is possible to grow house plants that will really bring your home to life with colour, foliage and form.

Potting on a houseplant

1 – Choose a pot that will happily accommodate the size of plant and will allow a little room for new growth. Place fresh compost in the base of the pot – a 50/50 mixture of peat alternative compost and loam compost is ideal for most houseplants as it will not dry out too quickly.

2 – Remove the plant from its plastic pot and position it in the new pot, taking care not to damage the root ball.

3 – Add more compost around the base of the plant, gently firming it in with your fingertips.

4 – Water the plant in thoroughly with a watering can. Regular watering is essential; with most houseplants, the important thing is never to let the compost dry out.

1

2

3

4

Houseplant hints & tips

Potting on When you buy a new house plant (usually in a plastic pot) pot it on to the next size up of pot, ideally not plastic. If you want to encourage the plant to increase in size, pot on every other year until the plant has attained the desired size. If you want to maintain the plant at roughly the size you bought it, keep it in the same size pot for longer.

Summer holidays Put house plants outdoors in summer, gradually acclimatizing them by putting them outside during the day and bringing them in at night. Don't put them in direct sunlight to start with.

Re-wetting If you forget to water a plant, or go away on holiday for example, and the compost does dry out, fill a jug or watering can with water and then add a few drops of washing-up liquid.

Correct positioning Make sure you position your house plants in the right locations. Many house plants do not light strong, direct sunlight, whilst others will thrive in the humid conditions found in a bathroom. Be sure to read the plant label and position the plant accordingly.

Pruning & Maintenance Techniques

A major part of the enjoyment that comes from having a garden is the feeling of fulfilment and satisfaction that comes from actively gardening. There are few, if any, ornamental plants that will perform to their best without some form of intervention, and in this chapter we will look at how to get the best from your garden by ensuring you are maintaining it correctly.

Pruning can often cause concern among the inexperienced gardener – why do plants need pruning, which ones should be pruned, how, when and why? Similarly, when is the best time of year to carry out border maintenance, and what does this constitute?

Taking care of the plants in your garden will make sure that they thrive for as long as possible, flower and fruit well, help to reduce the risks of pests and diseases and keep your garden looking in tip top condition. It is, after all, the very essence of gardening.

Pruning Trees & Shrubs

There are a variety of reasons for carrying out pruning on trees and shrubs: to increase flowering and fruiting, control disease or manipulate shape and size.

Pruning to maintain vigour

Shrubs such as Forsythia and *Viburnum farreri* need to have older wood pruned out annually to maintain vigour and the production of flowering wood. These are shrubs that produce new shoots from the base of the plant, which tend to produce more flower and fruit than the older wood. Left un-pruned they can soon become congested, the older wood reducing the opportunity for new shoots to form.

Every year after flowering cut out at the base around one third of the old wood.

Pruning for flower and fruit

A great many plants including ornamental fruit trees such as Malus (apple) will produce more flower and fruit when correctly pruned. *Buddleja davidii* will also flower more freely when pruned in the right way – hard pruning in spring.

As a general rule, plants that flower early in the season produce their flowering wood and buds during the previous growing year, while those that flower late in the season flower on that season's wood. Therefore, early flowering plants should be pruned as soon as they have finished flowering, while late season flowering plants can be pruned at the start of the growing season.

> **TIP**
>
> To maintain healthy plants it is essential to keep pruning out dead, diseased or damaged wood – the three Ds. In extreme cases fungal diseases can kill plants, while dead wood and damaged stems can form an entry point for disease and should be removed.

Pruning for foliage effect

There are a number of shrubs, such as the smoke bush (*Cotinus coggygria*), that can be manipulated through pruning, exchanging flowers and smaller leaves for no flowers but much enlarged leaves. This type of pruning is usually carried out in late winter or early spring and involves cutting the plant back quite hard, either to a framework of main branches, removing any twiggy growth, crossing branches and dead wood, or by cutting back to the ground.

Some trees can be hard pruned for foliage effect too, with specimens like the Indian Bean tree (*Catalpa bignonioides*) the Foxglove tree (*Paulownia tomentosa*) and the Tree of Heaven (*Ailanthus altissima*) being particularly suitable. This can totally change the dynamics of these plants, turning large flowering trees into plants with huge, lush foliage suitable for a sub-tropical planting or a foliage garden.

Pruning for stem colour

There are many shrubs that are grown for their stem colour effect, including varieties of Salix (willow), Cornus (dogwood) and Rubus. All of these plants require regular pruning if that colour is to be maintained.

Forsythia x *intermedia* 'Lynwood' with vigorous flowering shoots

Pruning tools

A great number of tools are available for pruning plants, but you are unlikely to need all of them. Here are just a few of the most commonly used items.

Secateurs [1] are used to prune soft shoots and small woody stems, employing either a scissors-like bypass cutting action or anvil cut. They are probably the most important garden tool, so it is worth investing in the best quality you can afford.

Loppers are used for pruning material that is too big to be cut with secateurs. As with secateurs, they are available with either bypass **[2]** or anvil **[3]** cut. Some have extendable arms, which are handy for pruning tall branches.

Pruning saws come in a variety of sizes and styles. The **Grecian saw [4]** is a small, one-handed saw with a sharply toothed, slightly curving blade. It makes short work of limbs too big for loppers, and is ideal for using in small, tight spaces. **Bow saws [5]** are used for larger branches and for felling small trees, and range from compact to very large two-person saws.

Ladders are useful for pruning taller shrubs and trees, but should be used with great care. A few pointers when using ladders:

• Do not use ladders on uneven ground.
• Never use ladders on your own.
• Do not overextend yourself when using ladders. If the ladder is too short either get a taller one for the job – or call a professional.
• If you feel unsafe on a ladder then the ladder is probably unsafe!

Usually this involves hard pruning close to the ground, 'coppicing', but with some plants – Salix in particular – a different effect can be achieved by allowing a single stem or trunk to form and then pruning the top growth back to this trunk, called 'pollarding'.

Coppicing This is a traditional woodland technique for producing wood which is suitable for fencing, tool handles and so on. By cutting the plant to the ground, long, straight stems form, ideal for practical applications. In the garden this technique is most often used to restrict size, and to promote fresh growth in trees and shrubs with colourful stems. Trees commonly coppiced include birch (Betula), hazel (Corylus), hornbeam (Carpinus), beech (Fagus) and sweet chestnut (Castanea).

Pollarding Often seen in towns and cities, pollarding involves the hard pruning of the tree crown back to a structure of main branches, to restrict overall size. Over the years these main branches form gnarled stumps. Pollarding also has its roots in woodland management.

Formative pruning

Formative pruning is all about achieving an attractive shape which will also limit potential weaknesses in growth. These can include crossing branches that rub against each other, and twin leaders – where instead of a single leading stem the plant develops two main shoots which compete with one another. This then leads to a pronounced fork forming between the two stems, which can be prone to rotting and splitting open, causing terrible damage.

The key to formative pruning is to achieve a natural, open shape avoiding congested branches to help with air circulation and healthy, pest-and-disease-free growth. At the same time, prune out any dead, diseased or damaged wood.

Renovation pruning

Sometimes older shrubs can get misshapen and woody, and you may be tempted to rip the plant out and start again. Before you do this always first consider renovation pruning – cutting the plant back quite hard to a decent framework. When doing this, try to retain some foliage on the lower stems and branches if possible, and after pruning give the plant a good feed and mulch to help boost chances of re-growth.

Correct Cuts

Using the correct pruning techniques is essential if the work you carry out is not to compromise the health of your plants.

Removing a branch

To remove a branch from a tree or shrub, first cut the branch back to within 30cm (12in) or so from the trunk. This will remove the weighty part of the branch and will prevent it from tearing.

The remaining stub can then be pruned closer to the trunk, but the cut should not be flush with the trunk. Instead, cut back to the swelling that occurs naturally where the branch extends from the trunk. This will then heal naturally by forming a callus over the cut.

It used to be common to seal pruning cuts with a 'wound paint' to aid healing, but this has now been proven to exacerbate problems with infection and actually inhibits the healing process.

Smaller branches When cutting back shorter branches, first make a cut underneath the branch close to where the final pruning cut will be [1]. Again, this will prevent tearing. Then carry out the final pruning cut at the swelling point of the branch [2 & 3].

General pruning

General pruning cuts on trees and shrubs should be made to a bud, which will then grow away without leaving a dead stump. Select a bud that is facing in the direction you want the branch to grow away to, usually outward facing, then make a slanting cut about 50mm (2in) above the bud; where the plant has opposing buds, cut straight across.

1

2

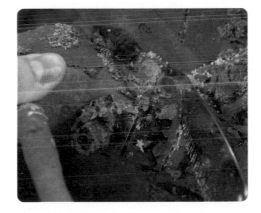

3

Pruning Hedges

Hedges are planted as windbreaks, boundary markers and security barriers – or they can be a decorative feature in their own right.

Basic technique

Hedges can be pruned with powered hedge trimmers or hand shears, with large leaved evergreen hedges benefiting from a tidy up with secateurs. Regenerative pruning or re-shaping will require the use of bow saws and loppers.

To achieve a really level finish to a formal hedge, set up a string line between two posts, the tops of which are the same distance from the ground – check this with a tape measure. Place the string line over the tops of the posts and make sure it is really taut, then use this line as a reference for the top of the hedge.

To create effects in hedges such as scalloped ends, use a wooden former or template made from plywood and mark the shape on the hedge with biodegradable line-marker spray paint.

When to prune

Evergreen hedges A hedge of box (*Buxus sempervirens*) will need trimming in early summer, ideally on a dry, overcast day when

Hedge trimming tips

A-shape Prune hedges to an A-shape, that is narrower at the top, to allow the base of the hedge to remain in light and consequently stay thick and healthy to the ground. In snowy areas, hedges pruned to an A-shape are less likely to collapse under the weight of the snow.

Large leaves Cut large-leaved evergreens with trimmers and then tidy them up with secateurs. Large leaves, when cut in half by trimmers, tend to die back and can become unsightly.

Birds' nests Always check for nesting birds before cutting hedges, and never cut in the main nesting season, from early spring to mid-summer.

Conifer hedges Do not prune coniferous hedges back too hard, that is into the woody growth, as, with the exception of yew, they will not regenerate.

the risk of the exposed cut foliage being scorched is reduced. Pruning box too early in the season will encourage unwanted extra growth which is sappy and soft and can be prone to frost damage. Other evergreen hedges – laurel for example, but excluding conifers – can be pruned in early autumn.

Coniferous hedges such as *Taxus baccata* (yew) should be pruned in late summer.

Deciduous hedges like beech (*Fagus sylvatica*) and hornbeam (*Carpinus betulus*) should be cut in late summer or early autumn.

Wildlife hedges including species that produce fruit or nuts that provide a source of winter food are best trimmed in early spring. Trim alternate sides of the hedge on alternate years to maximize the wildlife value.

String a line between two canes to ensure the hedge is level before you begin trimming

Pruning Roses

Roses tend to be the group of plants that create the greatest anxiety for gardeners when it comes to pruning. Conventional wisdom has it that anything other than precise cuts as prescribed by unwavering rules will spell disaster. Yet roses are far more resilient than is generally believed and will withstand a good deal of hacking about – they don't die easily!

The Basics

Rose pruning is often referred to as replacement pruning, because the object of the exercise is to replace old flowering wood with more vigorous new flowering wood. The best time to do this is winter or early spring when the rose plants are dormant.

Pruning to an outward bud In most cases, roses should be pruned to an outward facing bud, regardless of the type of rose. A bud is the growing point at which the plant produces leaves or shoots and during winter and early spring, the bud will usually be a modest swelling on the stem. The reason for pruning to an outward facing bud is to create a 'goblet' shaped plant with even growth all around. Too much growth in the centre will lead to congested stems and increase the risk of diseases, especially fungal diseases that thrive in conditions where air circulation is poor.

Pruning after planting Roses are best planted as bare root plants during the dormant season of winter or early spring. Soon after pruning the plant should be

pruned back hard to within five to eight buds from ground level, which will encourage strong new growth to form.

Autumn pruning Although the main pruning time for roses is winter and early spring, in exposed sites most roses will benefit from reduction in size by around a third in late autumn. This will prevent a phenomenon known as 'wind rock', whereby top-heavy plants are rocked back and forth by the winter winds, causing the plant to become unstable and risking damage to the stem and root system.

Careful and accurate pruning is preferable, but roses will stand harsher treatment than most people think

Pruning Different Types of Rose

Shrub roses After the first full season of growth, shrub roses will benefit from formative pruning. This is rather harder pruning than would take place in subsequent years, and should be aimed at improving the overall shape and structure of the plant. Thereafter, only modest pruning should take place during winter or early spring, pruning the previous season's growth back to a framework of outward

> **TIP** All roses will benefit from a proprietary rose feed applied after pruning. A good mulch of well rotted organic matter such as manure or garden compost will also aid re-growth, and during dry periods water plants well at the roots.

facing buds. Do not prune beyond the previous season's growth unless there is a need to remove dead, damaged or diseased material from the plant.

Bush and cluster-flowered These types of roses are the plants that require the hardest pruning of all in the rose family. They should be pruned back, to an outward facing bud, to within 5–8 buds from the ground during winter and early spring.

Climbing and rambling roses Rambling roses produce numerous shoots from ground level, and these should be pruned out, or 'replaced', on a regular basis by removing a third of the oldest stems every winter. Climbing roses produce lateral growth – effectively side shoots from the main stem that bear most of the flowering buds – from one or more main stems, and this lateral growth should be pruned back to a framework of outward facing buds. If this job is not undertaken regularly, many climbing roses will very quickly grow out of control and create problems.

Both types benefit from having flowering stems trained horizontally to assist the evenness of growth. In doing this the natural tendency for the plant to grow upwards is suppressed and instead more effort is put into producing flowering side shoots.

Take care of the thorns when pruning roses and wear gloves if you are not confident

Pruning Climbing Plants

Climbing plants include a wide range of plants with differing pruning requirements, but there are some general tips that can be applied across the group.

Spur Pruning

Spur pruning is a technique that can be applied to a range of plants such as the fruiting vines *Vitis vinifera* and *Vitis* 'Brant', ornamental vines including *Vitis coignetiae* and a range of other climbers including *Actinidia deliciosa* (Kiwi fruit). Although spur pruning is most often applied to vine-like fruiting plants, it is a technique that is equally suitable for many foliage effect vines.

The primary purpose of spur pruning is to create a framework of side shoots from which new flowering and fruiting wood can develop, while providing space within that framework for the fruit to develop fully. After flowering, or more usually during winter or early spring, create the spurs by reducing the side shoots to within three or four buds of the permanent framework.

Wisterias require two main pruning interventions; in late summer all the shoots

With spur pruning, cut back side shoots of fruiting or ornamental vines and other climbers to within three buds of the main lateral stem

Hedge trimmers would be the quickest method to cut back rampant-growing ivy

wildlife, the best time to carry out pruning is very early spring, when most of the fruits have gone but before the main nesting season for birds.

Pruning Clematis

There are three distinct groups of clematis that require different approaches:

Group one includes the early flowering clematis such as *C. alpina*, *C. armandii* and *C. montana*. Prune plants from this group after flowering, removing dead, damaged and diseased wood and reducing shoots.

Group two are the large flowered, mid-season flowering plants that include many popular cultivars like *C.* 'Nelly Moser' and *C.* 'Silver Moon'. In early spring before active growth begins, remove any dead, damaged or diseased shoots, and reduce the remaining stems back to a framework of strong buds.

Group three include later flowering clematis, *C.* 'Bill MacKenzie', *C. tangutica* and the many popular *C. viticella* hybrids; *C.* 'Etoile Violette', *C.* 'Polish Spirit' and so on. Prune clematis from this group hard back to within two to three buds from soil level.

(Wisterias produce many soft, long shoots) that are not required to create or enhance a flowering framework should be cut back to within 15cm (6in) of the main branches. In midwinter, spur pruning is applied, cutting back all the side shoots to within two or three buds of the main lateral stem.

Reduction Pruning

This is a simple technique for restricting the overall size of a climbing plant, and involves trimming the plant back to fit the space available. Carry out pruning during winter or early spring, cutting back side shoots to a bud.

In the case of vigorous plants like ivy (Hedera), the use of hedge shears or powered hedge trimmers will speed up the job. As ivy is a winter fruiting plant and provides much needed sustenance for

It is important to check which kind of pruning is suitable for the clematis growing in your garden

Indoor plants generally do not require much pruning, but check the individual plant's requirements

Foliage pruning

The timing of foliage pruning will to some extent be dictated by the type of plant, but in general old growth is pruned in autumn and new growth pruned during the growing season. The main method of foliage pruning for bonsai is known as finger pruning, and simply means the pinching out of foliage using the thumb and forefinger to help create a more balanced shape. Defoliation pruning is also common in bonsai training, and this involves removing between 60 and 90 per cent of the leaves in early summer. The leaves then re-emerge much smaller and often develop particularly intense autumn colour.

Root pruning

Root pruning is usually carried out every two to three years, sometimes annually, and helps to restrict growth and prevent the need for potting on, whilst at the same time ensuring the compost is replenished to provide adequate nutrients for the plant. During the dormant period of winter, the plant is carefully removed from its pot and the compost combed out from the roots. The larger, woody roots can then be cut back by between one third and a half, taking care not to damage or remove too many of the fine feeder roots. The plant should then be re-potted with fresh compost in its original pot, and watered in well.

Pruning Indoor Plants

In general, house plants need little pruning other than a little formative pruning and the removal of dead growth. Formative pruning usually consists of pinching out the growing tip of the plant to encourage bushy, compact growth. This is usually done using thumb and forefinger, pinching and twisting the growing tip – back to a bud – until it detaches, but can be done with sharp scissors or secateurs. This is usually carried out once the plant starts into active growth and begins producing lots of fresh growth.

Dead growth can be pruned out at any time, making sure to cut back to a living bud or stem, whilst dead leaves can usually be simply pulled off.

Pruning Bonsai

Bonsai pruning consists of two main elements: foliage pruning and root pruning. Added to that are the specialist techniques employed to artistically style bonsai, including the use of hand-held saws and drills to create deadwood effects, known as jins.

Although finger pruning is the prime method in foliage pruning, secateurs can also be used to artistically style bonsai

Border Maintenance

Keeping your ornamental borders in peak condition means ensuring that you are carrying out the right maintenance at the right time of year. In doing so not only will you ensure that your plants remain healthy and vigorous, you will also get the opportunity to really involve yourself in the yearly cycle of your garden and in doing so learn much more about the plants in it, and the conditions and cultural considerations that help to make them grow well.

Border maintenance offers the opportunity to put into practice much of the science of gardening that we have already looked at. Understanding how plants grow and the factors that influence their growth and health can really help when it comes to identifying and rectifying the sort of day-to-day problems that come about when maintaining garden plants. Knowing your soil well, for example, will inform when you carry out tasks such as mulching and plant division. The more you work in your garden, the greater the knowledge that you will accrue and more you will understand plants, gardens and gardening.

Late winter

- Continue pruning shrub, bush, climbing and rambling roses. Tie in ramblers and climbers to a climbing support, or to wires fixed to a wall or hedge (see page 70).
- Spur prune fruiting vines and foliage effect vines such as *Vitis coignetiae* (see pages 82–3).
- Remove the dead and diseased foliage from *Helleborus orientalis* and *Helleborus x hybridus*.
- Remove suckering growth from trees and shrubs such as *Tilia cordata* and *Cornus mas* (see pages 77–9).
- Remove the old foliage from Epimedium (barrenwort) cultivars to ensure the flowering stems show through.
- Harvest hazel (Corylus) and birch (Betula) poles for use as border plant supports. These 'poles' are either long straight stems or stems with twiggy side growth that are suitable for use when staking perennials (see page 68). They are harvested through coppicing or pollarding (see page 78). Always ask permission from the landowner if you are harvesting these from the countryside.
- Plant bare root roses (see pages 65–6).
- Prune native hedges that have provided fruit and nuts for wildlife over the winter months (see page 80).

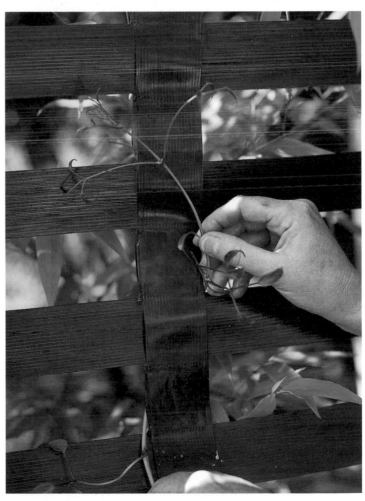

Tie in rambling and climbing plants to supports in late winter

Plant mid- to late flowering spring bulbs in the lawn

Early spring

- Prune foliage effect shrubs – such as *Cotinus coggygria* – back to a framework. Coppice or hard prune ornamental hazels including *Corylus maxima* 'Purpurea' and *Corylus avellana* 'Aurea', every three years or so (see page 77–8).
- Deadhead early flowering Mahonia by removing the flower spike back to the previous season's growth. If the plant is overgrown and leggy, cut back hard by removing up to half of the growth.
- Prune deciduous winter flowering Viburnum by removing up to a third of the old flowering wood (see page 77).
- Plant autumn flowering bulbs (see page 69).
- Prune stem colour shrubs, including *Cornus alba* cultivars, by hard pruning to within 20cm (8in) of the ground (see pages 77–8).
- Prune buddleja species and cultivars including *Buddleja davidii* and *Buddleja* x *weyeriana*. Prune back hard to a framework between 20cm (8in) and 1m (3ft) from the ground (see page 77).
- In conditions that are neither frozen nor waterlogged, cultivate new areas for planting (see pages 16–19).
- Cut back the spent flowering stems and foliage of perennials and grasses. This can also be done in autumn but the advantages of leaving this until spring are the attractiveness of the flowerheads and stems, and the enhanced biodiversity that comes from providing food and winter shelter for mammals, birds and bugs (see pages 14–15).
- Prune group 2 and 3 Clematis (see page 83).

Mid-spring

Once the risk of frosts has passed, prune the following:
- *Caryopteris clandonensis* cultivars and *Ceratostigma willmottianum* and *plumbaginoides*, back to a framework but not into the previous season's growth.
- *Perovskia* 'Blue Spire' to within 20–30cm (8–12in) from the ground.
- Silver foliage effect artemesia, including *Artemesia* 'Powis Castle', by trimming lightly.
- Send dried soil samples for testing and apply the correct fertilizer to counter any deficiencies that are confirmed (see pages 18–19).
- Mulch borders with composted organic matter, taking care not to mulch over the crowns of perennials or mulch around the stems of trees and shrubs (see page 17).
- Divide overgrown clumps of perennials and grasses, and replant or pot on (see page 94).
- Erect support systems for tall growing perennials by using birch or hazel poles and twine, or ready made support systems. Be sure to put these in place before any major growth takes place, in order to achieve a natural effect (see page 68).
- If you are happy using chemicals, start applying spray for blackspot and mildew on roses. This should be done before the leaf buds fully burst.

Divide overgrown perennials, grasses and sedges in mid-spring

Plant out annuals and half-hardy perennials once the risk of frost has passed in late spring

Mid- to late summer

- Deadhead euphorbia, remembering to wear gloves and goggles to prevent the sap from causing dermatitis or causing an eye injury.
- Clip box hedges (see page 80).
- Prune early flowering deciduous shrubs, after flowering, including forsythia and fragrant winter flowering viburnum (see page 77).
- Deadhead early flowering perennials such as *Geranium* 'Johnson's Blue' and *Nepeta* 'Six Hills Giant' by cutting back hard with hedge shears, which will encourage a second flush of flowers later in the season. Water well and apply a balanced liquid feed after pruning (see page 18).
- Deadhead repeat flowering roses to ensure they continue flowering, and remove leaves that are affected by blackspot including fallen leaves. These should be burned, not composted.
- Prune evergreen shrubs and begin trimming evergreen hedges and topiary (see page 80).
- Remove the spent flowers from French lavender as they go over.
- As taller perennials develop, increase the height of staking or plant supports to accommodate them (see page 65).
- Trim back the current season's growth of English lavender, before the flower buds form for the following season in late summer.
- Prune mid-season deciduous shrubs like Philadelphus (see page 77).
- Collect ripened seed from border plants for sowing.

Late spring and early summer

- Deadhead early flowering bulbs, such as daffodils, to prevent too much energy being expended on setting seed, but leave the foliage to die back naturally (see page 35).
- After flowering, prune group 1 flowering clematis (see page 83)
- Monitor the new, sappy growth of shrubs and perennials for aphids. If you are using chemicals, carefully apply according to the manufacturer's instructions. If not, wait for the natural predators to arrive, or for the non-squeamish, rub them off using thumb and forefinger (see page 147).
- If frost is likely, protect the flower buds of wisteria with horticultural fleece.
- Tie in the growing stems of climbers such as clematis and climbing roses (see page 70).
- Plant out hardy plants including perennials and shrubs.
- Plant out annuals and half hardy perennials, once the risk of late frost has passed.
- Keep on top of weeding, especially perennial weeds (see pages 17 and 152–4).
- Remove the dead foliage of early and mid-season flowering bulbs and feed with a balanced fertilizer.

Collect ripened seed for sowing from border plants at the height of summer

Check staking and tree ties in autumn, ahead of harsh winter weather

Watering tips

Water has a huge part to play in any garden, essential to the growth of all plants. Not only is it essential to garden plants, it is a globally precious, and frequently scarce resource. With predicted climate change and increasingly erratic weather becoming a reality, the responsible use of water by gardeners is vitally important.

Follow these tips to ensure that you make the best use of water in your garden:

- Do not water at the start of the growing season. This can be difficult in a dry spring when plants are, seemingly, refusing to grow. But watering at this time is the worst thing you can do, as once you have started you will have to carry on! Be patient and wait for rain before you resort to watering.
- Little and often is a disaster! Plants need deep watering when they are under stress, which can mean 15 minutes of water at a good flow rate per plant. A few seconds of water will only damp down the soil and encourage the plant roots to grow to the surface in search of moisture, where they will be even more vulnerable to drying out.
- Water when the sun goes down. With lower air temperatures evaporation is dramatically reduced, and there is no chance of scorching foliage or flowers.
- Try not to use sprinklers, as they are the least efficient way of irrigating. On a hot day up to 85% of the water will evaporate before it even touches the ground – let alone get taken up by the plant! If you have to use sprinklers do so at night.
- Consider installing an automated watering system. It will water your plants efficiently and cost effectively.
- Flood the place... One of the most efficient ways to irrigate is to lay a running hose on the border and periodically move it, usually at ten to fifteen minute intervals. This is referred to as 'flooding' and has the benefit of ensuring plenty of water gets to the plants without the need to stand around holding a hose.
- If you have to, sacrifice your lawn! Lawns will almost always regenerate, no matter how dead they look.

Autumn

- Lift and divide perennials, if required (see page 94).
- Replant existing plants that are incorrectly positioned either because of height, colour or cultural considerations.
- Reduce shrub roses and buddleja by up to one third to reduce wind rock (see page 81).
- Before the soil becomes damp and cold, autumn provides a second opportunity for mulching (see page 17).
- Plant spring flowering bulbs (see pages 68–9).
- Plant perennials, grasses, shrubs and trees and in particular bare root plants from these groups (see page 63).
- Check staking and tree ties on recently planted trees to ensure that they are not so tight as to be 'strangling' the tree, and adjust as required by moving the collar of the tree tie to a point where it supports the tree without biting into the bark (see page 65).
- Trim deciduous hedges that are not being grown for their wildlife benefits, that is those that produce berries and nuts (see page 80).
- Prune wisteria.
- Collect late ripening seed for sowing.

Early to mid-winter

- Begin pruning roses (see pages 81–2).
- Crown lift trees and shrubs (see page 10).
- Remove dead, damaged and diseased wood from woody plants (see page 77).
- Continue planting – especially bare root trees and shrubs – until weather conditions preclude it (see pages 63–5).

Propagation Techniques

There are all sorts of ways to obtain plants for your garden, from conventional garden centres and nurseries to exchanging plants with other gardeners. One of the most rewarding, however, must be growing your own plants, from seeds, cuttings, layers and so on. A commercial nursery growing plants by the thousand will have all sorts of specialist equipment to propagate and grow on plants until they are large enough to sell. However, many plants can be propagated with comparative ease in your own home and without the need for lots of expensive kit.

The advantages of growing your own plants are many. If you are propagating from existing plants in your own garden, then you will already know that the plant can cope with the prevalent conditions, so the risk factor is removed. The most obvious advantage is cost, as a few failed seeds or cuttings are a lot easier to cope with than the loss of big expensive plants. The factor that recommends home propagation above all other considerations is that it is a stimulating and fun way to learn more about gardening. There are few more satisfying experiences in gardening than nurturing to maturity a plant that you have grown from seed or cutting.

In this chapter we will look at a variety of methods of plant propagation that are suitable to try out at home, plus a number of more challenging techniques that can be attempted with a little more experience – or just a sense of adventure!

Growing From Seed

Growing plants from seed is a great way of producing a lot of plants for little cost. However, it does require effort in the early stages to ensure that seedlings are not affected by the fungal diseases caused by inadequate ventilation and too much humidity.

Tools and equipment for propagating

Although home propagation does not require the same level of equipment as that needed for commercial growing, a basic set of tools and equipment is essential:

- **A sharp knife** is absolutely essential. Do not forget to buy a wet stone in order to keep the knife sharp.
- **Pots and trays** for sowing seed and inserting cuttings.
- **Hormone rooting powder or liquid** Hormone treatments are used to boost the rooting potential of cuttings.
- **Composts and compost admixtures** such as horticultural sand, vermiculite and grit.
- **A propagator** These devices provide heat to the base of cuttings through an electrical coil.
- **A cold frame** These can either be purchased from a supplier or made quite simply at home.

To sow seed in a pot, hold it in the palm of your hand and scatter it gently across the growing medium

Sowing Seed Indoors or Under Glass

Prepare a seed tray by filling it with appropriate compost and giving the whole tray base a sharp tap on a table top. This will help to settle the compost, but it should then be further firmed by using a flat, level piece of wood, ideally exactly half the width but the full length of the tray.

Next, a few questions about the seed that you are sowing:
- Does the seed require direct light? If so, sow the seed directly onto the surface of the compost
- Should the seed be sown in a drill? (This is a shallow trench that is then covered over). If so, check the depth required and form the drill.
- Does the seed need to be surface sown and then covered in sand?

Once you have sown the seed, water well with a watering can fitted with a rose. Then place the tray in a propagator to provide bottom heat. Monitor the tray and do not let the compost dry out.

Pricking out

As the seed germinates, cotyledons (seed leaves) will form. Once these have developed to the point that they can handled, the seedlings should be pricked out. This means thinning out the emerging seedlings – removing some – to give the others enough room to develop.

1 – Prepare a tray of suitable growing medium.
2 – Gently remove individual seedlngs from the original pot using a dibber.
3 – Make holes with a dibber in the new tray of compost and re-plant the seedlings, spreading them evenly and ensuring that they have sufficient room to establish and develop comfortably.
4 – When the tray of growing medium is full of seedlings, place it in a greenhouse or propagator and leave the seedlings to develop.

1

2

3

4

TIP

If you are collecting a lot of cutting material, place it in a plastic bag and seal the top, but remember to use a different bag for each plant – or you could end up with some very unusual results!

Potting on

Once the seedlings have developed into small plants and have established a good root system they can be potted on into individual pots, or several plants can be potted into a large pot.

Sowing Seed Outdoors

Sowing seed outdoors is remarkably straightforward, but does require time being spent on cultivating the soil to a fine tilth, which is achieved by digging over the soil and then raking over several times in different directions to remove or break down large lumps. Once the soil has been worked to a fine crumb texture with no large lumps or stones, two different methods can be used.

Sowing in drills

This type of sowing is best for vegetables or plants being grown for transplanting.
1 – Create a shallow drill with a dibber.
2 – Sow the seed at the recommended rate by taking a pinch of seed between thumb and forefinger and drizzling the seed into the drill.
3 – Back fill the drill with soil and water in well with a watering can fitted with a fine rose. Once the seedlings have developed, prick them out as described above.

Broadcast sowing

Broadcast sowing usually takes place in early spring, and is suitable for ornamental annuals, cornfield annuals and so on. The seed can be sown directly onto the soil, or onto a thin layer of gravel mulch spread onto the soil (which helps to prevent rot and suppresses weeds).

1

2

3

Growing From Cuttings

The majority of woody plants available to buy from nurseries and garden centres have been grown from cuttings. Although the range of plants that can be grown from cuttings at home is, understandably, not as wide as can be grown with specialist equipment, there are many useful and attractive plants that can be propagated with comparative ease.

There are four main ways in which cuttings can be prepared to be struck that are suitable for home propagation:

- Nodal cuttings are made by making the cut directly below the leaf joint.
- Internodal cuttings are made by making the cut between two leaf joints.
- Heeled cuttings are made by tearing side shoots from the main stem. The resultant heel is then trimmed with a knife before inserting into the growing media.
- Basal cuttings are side shoots taken from the main parent branch by cutting with a sharp knife through the slight swelling where the two meet.

Taking & planting cuttings

Cuttings should be collected at the appropriate time (usually spring) from a representative part of the parent plant.

Hardening off and planting out

Regardless of the type of cutting method you employ, once rooted cuttings have been potted on they should be gradually hardened off for a few weeks, by placing outside (or lifting the light on the cold frame) during the day and then returning to a sheltered spot at night. The time between potting on and planting out will depend entirely on the species of plant, so while buddlejas are likely to be ready to plant out the first season after cutting, camellias will probably need two or more seasons of growing on, and perhaps one more pot-on, before they can be planted.

1 – Before inserting the cuttings, make a new, clean cut with secateurs or a sharp knife, and remove all but the top three or four leaves, so that at least two thirds of the cutting is clear stem. In some cases it is recommended that you wound the cutting, which involves removing a grape skin thickness slice from the side of the stem, down to the cut.

2 – Make sure that the bottom of the cutting is cut off neatly.

3 – Dip the base of the cutting into hormone rooting powder, shaking off any surplus. Rooting hormones help to promote rooting and come in either powder or liquid forms. Commercial nurseries would only use rooting hormones on plants that absolutely need it, but on a domestic level they are more easily justified. Try experimenting with cuttings taken from the same plant, wounding and treating some, treating but not wounding others and so on. You will soon be able to assess which method works the best for a variety of subjects.

4 – When you are inserting cuttings into the growing media, use a pencil or dibber to firm the compost around the base of the cutting.

1

2

3

4

A propagator is a wise investment if you plan to take lots of cuttings, but plastic bags placed over pots will usually serve the same purpose

Insert to about a third of their overall length, and at three or four to a pot for larger pots (1ltr/2pt or more) or singly or in threes for smaller, 9cm (4in) pots. If you are planting cuttings into trays rather than pots, insert the cuttings so that their foliage is only just touching the compost.

Softwood cuttings

Softwood cuttings are taken early in the growing season when the growing tips of plants are still soft. They are the hardest of all cuttings to strike (get to root) in a domestic environment because without bottom heat from a propagator and regular misting, which can only be achieved with a specialist mist unit, they rapidly wilt and die.

Semi-ripe cuttings

These are usually basal or nodal cuttings that are taken at a point when the growth has begun to harden off, usually during early to mid-summer. Cuttings taken at this time are best struck in one of two ways, using either a cold frame or pot.

Cold frame method

The cold frame and plastic method uses a standard cold frame with the base covered with a 20cm (8in) layer of either pure horticultural sand (non-calcareous sand with even particle size) or horticultural sand mixed with a loam based compost. The sand is important to ensure good drainage, and

has the advantage that it warms up quickly helping the roots to establish more rapidly.

Begin by inserting prepared cuttings in rows into the growing media and watering in. Cover over the cold frame with a clear, light gauge plastic secured at all sides, then replace the cold frame light (the glazed frame that covers the cold frame); the plastic helps to keep humidity levels up and reduce wilting. Once the cuttings have begun to root, gradually remove the plastic, at first by lifting the sides, then folding back for part of the day and finally removing it completely. During periods when frost is a risk, replace the light and cover with sacking or horticultural fleece.

Pot method

Refer to the sequence on the opposite page for how to plant the cuttings into pots. Ensure that the plants are well watered in and then place a clear plastic bag over the pot, secured with a rubber band. This will help to prevent wilting and increase humidity. Place the pot on a warm window sill or into a propagator, checking regularly for root growth. As the roots start to develop remove the plastic bag in stages, as with the cold frame and plastic method.

Hardwood cuttings

Hardwood cuttings are harvested in late autumn or winter from mature wood.
1 – Dig a shallow trench (18cm/7in).
2 – Take cuttings and dip their ends in hormone powder.
3 – Insert the cuttings into a sand or sand-mixed media.
4 – Back-fill the trench with soil and check the cuttings periodically.

1

2

3

4

Propagating by Division

Dividing plants is a straightforward way of propagating many perennial plants, and has the added benefit of reinvigorating old clumps of perennials that are no longer producing foliage and flowers as they would if they were in full health.

In spring or autumn, lift clumps of perennials and grasses by digging them out and placing them on a level surface such as a board or sheet of plastic.

Using a pair of digging forks placed back to back, tease the clump apart into evenly sized smaller pieces. If the clump is very old and woody, use a sharp knife or a spade with a good edge to cut the clump into smaller sections.

Once the clump of plants has been divided, discard the centre section if it is congested and woody, and plant out or pot on the divided sections, remembering to water them in well to help them establish.

Division of woody perennials is easily effected with two forks

Propagating by Layering

Layering is a great way to propagate woody plants without the use of any specialist equipment. Many plants layer themselves naturally, laying down their lower branches until they make contact with the soil and root. Layering takes advantage of this tendency to produce more plants.

Simple layering can be carried out either in early spring when the parent plant is still in its dormant state, or in late summer when the wood is mature. Find an appropriate flexible stem and dig a shallow trench close

An ivy (Hedera) stem from the parent plant pinned down in a pot of compost for simple layering

to the parent plant. Bend the stem down into the trench and pin it with a U shaped length of wire, leaving 15–20cm (6–8in) of growth still above ground. Scrape away a thin layer of bark from the stem using a sharp knife. This will increase the chances of rooting by exposing the cambium to the soil. Periodically check the layer to ensure the soil does not dry out and to check on the development of roots. After a full season, the layer should be ready to detach from the parent plant, and can then be either planted out or potted on.

Air Layering

Air layering can be used on a range of woody plants, including many that are hard to propagate at home using other methods.

1 – In spring, select a stem on the plant you wish to propagate that is at least as thick as your little finger. About 30cm (1ft) from the end of the stem, and just below a node, use a sharp knife to cut a ring all the way around the stem that is as deep as the bark. Cut a second ring parallel with the first and about 2.5cm (1in) away, joining the two rings together with a third cut. Peel the bark away to expose the cambium and use a knife to scrape some of the cambium away, in doing so preventing the wound from callusing over.

2 – Cut the bottom from a polythene bag and place the tube over the stem.

3 – Pack out the exposed wound with growing media – traditionally moistened sphagnum moss (as shown), but wood shavings or coir fibre can also work.

4 – Hold the moss in place with black plastic wrapped around the stem and securely tied.

1

2

3

4

Agave americana frequently produces offsets from its base

Propagating From Plantlets

Another very simple means of propagation involves taking advantage of the natural habit of some plants to produce plantlets. These small offsets, miniatures of the parent plant, are usually formed as satellites of the parent, and are often referred to variously as offsets, bulblets or cormlets depending on whether the parent is perennial, bulb or corm. These 'baby plants' can be simply detached from the parent and either potted on or planted out.

Bulbs and corms In the case of bulbous plants and corms, including narcissus and cyclamen, propagating this way should be done during their dormant season, the bulb or corm being lifted from the ground and the bulblet or cormlet removed. The parent can then be replanted and will benefit from an application of balanced fertilizer and a good watering.

Perennials In the case of perennials producing plantlets, such as *Agave americana* and *Eryngium agavifolium*, the offsets can be detached using a sharp knife, carefully lifted and replanted or potted. It is a good idea to do this in early autumn, when you are less likely to injure the plant.

Growing Plants for Food

Growing your own food is possibly the single most rewarding aspect of gardening. The knowledge that the food on your plate is the product of your own endeavour and the method of its growth entirely controlled by you – weather not withstanding – holds a great appeal for many gardeners. The attractiveness of 'home grown' food has become heightened in recent years by increasing concerns over modern farming methods and the use of pesticides and herbicides, with the development of genetically modified crops further adding to the feeling of uncertainty and worry over where our food comes from.

Once you start growing your own food you begin to appreciate the seasonal nature of food – something we have lost in recent years due to the supermarket culture. A sweet, ripe strawberry picked at the right time from your own plot will be simply light years ahead of an imported strawberry that has been forced on in a greenhouse and tastes of little more than water. And anyway, who wants to eat strawberries in winter? Surely the whole point of fruit and vegetables is enjoying the anticipation of a crop coming into season, just as we used to do as recently as 20 years ago?

Nowadays, we are used to having a wide variety of food available all year round, but apart from the country of origin it is almost impossible to know anything about the way in which it has been produced. Growing your own food is enjoyable and highly rewarding, and removes the uncertainty that can come from buying food.

Growing Vegetables

You do not need a dedicated vegetable garden to grow edible plants, as it is easy to incorporate vegetables into an ornamental garden, especially those with attractive foliage such as salad crops and Swiss chard or those with flowers, like chives. Containers and windowboxes can also be used to grow vegetables, with tomatoes, capsicums (sweet peppers and chilli peppers) and even potatoes being suitable for this kind of cultivation.

Site and Soil

The best site for growing vegetables is one that is open and sunny with good air circulation, but sheltered from strong winds which can reduce plant growth through desiccation and 'wind pruning'. A site that slopes gently towards the sun will warm more quickly than a level site, making it ideal for bringing on early crops.

As with all plants, it is important to ensure thorough soil cultivation, but with vegetables it is perhaps even more vital, as the quality and fertility of the soil has a direct bearing on the growth rates, size and flavour of the vegetables themselves. With edible crops it is very much the case that you get out what you put in, so annual soil improvement by digging in well rotted manure or garden compost is essential (see pages 15–19).

Good soil On sites with a good depth of topsoil, use the double or single digging techniques to improve the soil, working in plenty of well rotted manure, garden compost, green manure or spent mushroom compost.

Poor soil If the soil quality is poor, then it is well worth considering making raised beds, the bottom of which can be filled with manure or compost before topping up with soil.

How to get started

If you are setting out to grow your own food in your garden, it is worth remembering these few tips:

- **Grow what you want to eat** It sounds obvious, but sometimes it is easy to be tempted into growing plants that you think you should grow, rather than those that you actually enjoy eating!
- **Start small** It is better to get a feel for how to grow edible plants and gradually build up from there. Underestimating the time commitment required can turn what should be an enjoyable adventure into a chore.
- **Work out how much you need to grow** A family of four will, of course, require more food than a couple or single person. Decide whether your plot will supplement purchased fruit and vegetables or whether you intend to aim for self-sufficiency.
- **Learn from others** If there is a gardening club in your local area, go along to one of their meetings. You will find a wealth of knowledge on hand and plenty of practical advice.

There is great satisfaction to be had from growing your own vegetables

Planning Your Plot

Once you have selected the site for your vegetable plot and worked out the space available you will have a clearer idea of the amount and variety of veg you can grow. Sit down with a piece of paper (graph paper is ideal as you can translate measurements easily from the ground) and work out the layout of your plot. Bear in mind the following:

Access You will need to include paths in your design wide enough to push a wheelbarrow around and so that you are not stepping on crops to get at others. Use crushed stone, paving slabs or simply dress the soil with a layer of bark.

Practicalities Vegetable plots need to be easy to manage and productive. Row cropping is the traditional method of growing straight rows of crops that are easy to sow, thin, weed and harvest.

Companion planting

Companion planting is one way of reducing pest damage and is achieved by using plants that mask or confuse the scent of the crop, causing the pest to be disorientated – or disinterested! Crops can be also be used to 'nurse' other crops, providing shelter as well as masking the scent of the crop.

- **French marigolds** planted alongside tomatoes will deter whitefly.
- **Sunflowers** provide excellent shade for growing cucumbers, or peas and beans will do the same job.
- **Legumes (peas and beans)** can be interplanted with brassicas that will benefit from the nitrogen fixing nodules on the roots of legumes. After harvesting, dig the remains of the plants into the soil to act as a green manure. Swedes and turnips will also benefit from growing alongside.
- **Broad/runner beans** these are good nurse crops for sweetcorn and potato seedlings.
- **Celery** grows well with leeks but will also deter the Large White (or Cabbage White) butterfly from attacking brassicas.
- **Garlic** grows well with lettuce and beetroot, and helps deter aphid attack.

Appearance As well as being productive, vegetable plots can also be beautiful in their own right. The French developed the idea of the potager, an ornamental vegetable garden where edible crops are displayed in an aesthetically pleasing way, particularly suited to smaller spaces.

Crop rotation

The practice of rotating crops around your vegetable plot has a number of advantages. It prevents the build up of pests and diseases

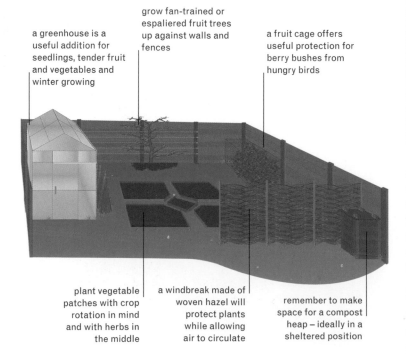

a greenhouse is a useful addition for seedlings, tender fruit and vegetables and winter growing

grow fan-trained or espaliered fruit trees up against walls and fences

a fruit cage offers useful protection for berry bushes from hungry birds

plant vegetable patches with crop rotation in mind and with herbs in the middle

a windbreak made of woven hazel will protect plants while allowing air to circulate

remember to make space for a compost heap – ideally in a sheltered position

associated with particular crops and ensures that nutrients remain balanced in the soil – some crops demand particular nutrients more than others and can leave the soil depleted if the crop is not rotated. By clearing and rotating the beds within your vegetable plot annually, you will also be able to control weeds more easily.

Vegetables are usually classified into four groups for the purposes of crop rotation:

- Legumes (peas and beans)
- Brassicas (cabbage, broccoli, Brussels sprouts, cauliflower)
- Onion family (onions, shallots, garlic, spring onions, leeks, also courgettes and lettuce)
- Carrot/Tomato family (including potatoes, parsnips and other root vegetables, aubergines and peppers)

These groups should be rotated annually to

TIP
If you have enough space you might consider having a 'spare' plot, so that out of five available plots only four are being used at any one time. This allows one plot to be 'rested' for a season which can further help to reduce soil borne pests and diseases from building up in the vegetable garden as a whole.

ensure that the same group is not in the same plot for consecutive years. A typical crop rotation regime could consist of:

Bed 1 – Carrot/Tomato family
Bed 2 – Brassicas
Bed 3 – Legumes
Bed 4 – Onion family

with each group following the other over a four-year period, so that in the second year the onions would move to bed 1, carrot and tomatoes to bed 2, brassicas to bed 3 and legumes to bed 4.

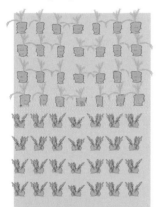

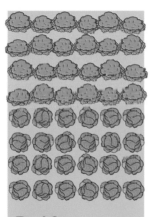

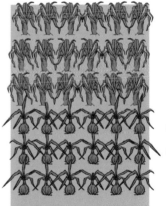

Bed 1: Carrot/ Tomato family

Vegetables:
Aubergine; beetroot; carrot; parsnip; pepper; potato; swede; turnip; tomato; sweet potato

Care:
Double digging; liberal application of blood, fish and bonemeal before planting

Bed 2: Brassicas

Vegetables:
Cabbage; Chinese cabbage; Brussels sprouts; cauliflower; kale; calabrese; broccoli

Care:
Single digging; mixing manure in soil; application of blood, fish and bonemeal

Bed 3: Legumes

Vegetables:
Broad bean; French bean; Lima bean; pea; runner beans; yard long bean; asparagus pea

Care:
Single digging; mixing lime in soil; application of blood, fish and bonemeal

Bed 4: Onions

Vegetables:
Bulb onion; shallot; garlic; spring onion; pickling onion; Welsh onion; leek; Japanese bunching onion

Care:
Double digging; mixing manure in soil; application of blood, fish and bonemeal

Intercropping and catch cropping

Intercropping is a way of maximizing your growing space by utilizing the 'spare' soil between slow growing crops to raise plants that can later be transplanted into their final cropping positions. For example, rows of broad beans can be intercropped with cos lettuce, the lettuce being either harvested in situ or transplanted at an early stage to its own plot. Intercropping is only really successful when the crops involved do not compete too much with each other, so tap rooted plants like carrots and parsnips are best intercropped with brassicas for transplanting. Annuals grown for flower cutting can make a good intercrop, and can help to reduce pest attack of

TIP

To prevent having an excess of crops one week and nothing the next, sowing in succession with evenly timed gaps between each sowing will ensure a regular quantity of harvestable crops throughout the season. This method is particularly useful for salad crops, which mature quickly but do not store well.

insects such as the carrot root fly by creating a barrier around the carrots.

Catch crops are those that grow from seed to maturity quickly, and are therefore suitable for growing in the space where a main crop will later be planted. Catch crops include salad onions, lettuce and rocket.

Raised beds

Raised beds are particularly useful if your soil is poor and/or shallow, as it allows for the depth of soil to be increased. They can also be very helpful for people with limited mobility, as the bed height can be made to allow easy access from a wheelchair, for example. Raised beds can be constructed from bricks or blocks, but are quick and cost-effective to build from untreated railway sleepers or heavy gauge plywood.

Sowing Vegetables

Before any sowing takes place, the seedbed should be prepared by raking over to a fine tilth and removing any large stones. Depending on the crop, seed should be sown in drills (a shallow, narrow trench in the soil) varying from a few millimetres deep to a few centimetres. Seed can either be sown at a rate greater than required and then thinned out, which is handy for crops that are prone to pest damage, or sown at the desired crop rate and not thinned.

Sowing 'under glass'

Crops can also be started off indoors under glass in pots, trays or small planting modules and then hardened off before planting out when the risk of frost has passed. This allows the crop to reach the harvesting stage much earlier than would be normal. 'Soft' crops such as salad leaves benefit from this method, as do beetroot, pepper and chilli. Other crops can be grown in cloches (miniature glasshouses that are placed over the crop outdoors to provide frost protection and increase temperatures) or in polytunnels or under horticultural fleece to provide an early harvest. Garlic, swede and turnip can all be grown or started off in this way.

An Introduction to Vegetables

For most gardeners the starting point for all productive gardening is growing vegetables. The range and diversity of this group of plants means that there are now vegetables for every single month of the year, even during the notorious 'hungry gap' of winter when, historically, few vegetables were available to harvest and eat.

This is not just because of new varieties that have been bred, but also as a consequence of the introduction of exotic vegetables from all over the world. Alongside these excitingly different vegetables comes an understanding of how to cook and use them, making this perhaps the most exciting time ever to be growing your own vegetables.

Salad Plants

Salad vegetables include lettuce, mustard and cress, endive and rocket and are those crops that are grown for their fresh, tasty salad leaves. They are mostly annuals and can be grown from seed to cropping in a comparatively short space of time.

Leaf lettuce

Leaf lettuce are the 'cut and come again' types that grow without producing an obvious heart and can be cut regularly to the ground or have single leaves removed. Popular cultivars include the slightly bitter 'Lollo Rossa' and 'Lollo Blonda', both of which have decorative leaves. The cultivar 'Salad Bowl' is an old form but an excellent one, producing plenty of good, crisp leaves, whilst 'Oak Leaf' would make an excellent front of border bedding plant with its colourful leaves.

Lettuce 'Lollo Rossa'

Lettuce

Lettuce are usually divided into three main groups, within which there are many cultivars:
• Leaf lettuce
• Cabbage lettuce
• Cos lettuce

Cabbage lettuce

Cabbage lettuce are heart forming lettuce with good resistance to drought. The two main types are Butterhead, summer grown lettuce with buttery leaves, and the crisp and crunchy Crisphead types. Butterhead cultivars include 'All Year Round', 'Buttercrunch', the virus and mildew resistant 'Action' and the high yielding and heat resistant 'Avondefiance'. For something a little different, try 'Sangria', with red tinged outer leaves. Among the Crisphead cultivars are the famous 'Iceberg', the fast growing 'Malika' and the popular and reliable 'Webb's Wonderful'.

Lettuce 'Iceberg'

Cos lettuce

Cos lettuce require rich, moist soils and a good supply of water. They take longer to reach harvesting stage than cabbage lettuce so can be a useful component in a successional scheme. The compact 'Little Gem' and late cropping 'Winter Density' are just two of the many good Cos cultivars.

Lettuce Cos 'Little Gem'

Lettuce care

Sow:	From late winter in pots under glass or with the protection of a cold frame from mid-spring. Protect outdoor sowings with, for example, cloches or fleece until seedlings establish. Sow in succession.
Crop:	Harvest Cabbage and Cos lettuce from early summer, leaf lettuce as early as four weeks after sowing.
Care:	Water well during dry periods.
Pests and diseases:	In cool, damp weather Botrytis mould can affect lettuce. This can be treated with a fungicide, or alternatively grow resistant varieties. Root aphid can cause stunted growth or total collapse of the plant. Affected plants should be destroyed.

Cucumber and squash care

Sow:	From mid-spring in a propagator or under glass at 20–25°C (35–44°F), or from late spring in an unheated glasshouse.
Crop:	From mid-summer to early autumn, ensuring the fruit are fully ripe before picking.
Care:	Water well during dry periods and mist regularly, feed with a high potash fertilizer every two weeks. Remove the male flowers of indoor cultivars but not those of outdoor varieties (they need them for insect pollination). Female flowers differ from male flowers in that they have a swelling behind the flower.
Pests and diseases:	Cucumber mosaic virus causes mottled, distorted leaves, affected plants should be burned. Aphid, red spider mite and slugs can attack plants.

Squashes

Squashes include courgette, marrow, pumpkin, zucchini, cucumber and those squashes grown for their ornamental rather than culinary value. Squashes have been in cultivation for thousands of years and many are valued for being edible whether raw or cooked, as well as their decorative value. The seeds of many of the plants in this group can be valuable to health as they are rich in zinc.

Cucumbers

Cucumbers are climbing annual plants, grown in a greenhouse or outdoors and producing fruit that are variously long and sausage shaped or rounded. These include pickling varieties, normally referred to as gherkins.

Greenhouse cultivars need temperatures of around 20°C (35°F) and a humid atmosphere, with humus rich soil that drains well but does not dry out. Outdoor plants must be sown and grown on under glass and as the seedlings develop they should be tied up to canes and gradually hardened off before planting out once the risk of frost has passed. Cucumbers can be grown on cane tripods, against trellis or on wires attached to posts.

Sliced cucumber is a staple of summer salads

Outdoor cucumber 'Burpless Tasty Green F1'

Greenhouse cultivars Many greenhouse cultivars are sold as being all female, due to the fact that pollination between male and female flowers causes the cucumbers to taste bitter. Greenhouse cucumbers include the smooth skinned 'Telegraph' and the unusual, rounded 'Crystal Apple'.

Outdoor cultivars For cool climates, 'Marketmore' is a good cultivar, 'Crystal Lemon' and 'Athene' make good pickling cucumbers, and 'Long Green Improved' is a tough, productive plant.

Squashes

Squashes are either bushy or trailing/climbing annuals, some of which are extremely vigorous. Among the most decorative squashes are the winter squashes and pumpkins, the flesh of which is extremely tasty when cooked. Some of these squashes are truly massive, with 'Atlantic Giant' being known to grow to over 300kg (660lb). 'Buttercup' is a more manageable choice, with firm, tasty flesh.

Marrows are simply elongated squashes, and perhaps the most versatile is 'Tender and True', which is disease resistant and can be picked when young and used as a courgette.

Courgette and Zucchini are marrows that have been bred specifically for picking when small, such as 'Gold Rush' and 'Supremo'.

Winter squash 'Sweet Dumpling'

Onion Family

The onion – or Allium – family members are among the oldest and longest cultivated of all culinary plants. They include leeks, onions, shallots and garlic.

Onion

Onions are divided into three groups; the common bulb onions, pickling onions and spring or salad onions. All need a sunny site and well drained, fertile soil to thrive. The easiest way to grow bulb and pickling onions is to buy and plant 'sets', immature bulblets that are grown by suppliers for this purpose. Whether you are growing from sets or seedlings, successional sowing should be employed to keep up a constant supply. Because bulb and pickling onions are comparatively easy to store and keep, over-production should not cause problems. Crop rotation is essential when cultivating onions.

Bulb onions

Bulb onions include the well known 'Ailsa Craig', with good size and a mild taste, the red onion 'Red Baron', which has a much stronger flavour, and the high cropping 'Sturon'.

Onion 'Ailsa Craig'

Pickling onions

Pickling onions are smaller in size than other culinary onions and should remain firm when pickled, and the timing of harvesting is important for pickling onions if they are not to get too large or woody. They must be peeled thoroughly prior to storing, if they are not being pickled immediately after harvesting. 'Paris Silverskin' is a popular cocktail pickle that is very tolerant of poor soil and dry conditions. The variety 'Shakespear' is a well flavoured small pickling onion.

Onion 'Paris Silverskin'

Onion care

Sow:	Bulb and pickling onions in spring and again in autumn, but better to grow from sets which mature more quickly. Sow spring onions thinly in drills.
Crop:	Harvest bulb and pickling onions as soon as leaves begin to dry. Harvest spring onions at any stage, even the thinned seedlings are good for salads.
Care:	Lime acid soils before planting or sowing, water well during dry periods.
Pests and diseases:	If onion root fly larvae is a problem, grow from sets and employ crop rotation.

Spring onions

Spring onions are usually grown for flavouring salads or quick cooking dishes such as stir-fry. Popular varieties include the hardy 'Winter-Over', late sown in the autumn for an early crop, the mild tasting 'Winter White Bunching', which has noticeably slim stalks and 'Beltsville Bunching', a variety which tolerates hot, dry conditions. Particularly good for their ornamental value in salads are those spring onions with colourful stems, such as 'Redmate', which has a red tinge to the base of its stems, and 'Santa Claus', which is especially red in colder weather.

Onion 'White Lisbon'

Parsnips

Parsnips take eight to nine months from sowing to harvesting and require deep, well worked neutral to slightly alkaline soil, and so are not a crop that every gardener will attempt to grow. They are grown from seeds which take time to germinate and so it is common practice to sow radish seeds between the parsnips to help mark where they are. Keep the crop regularly watered and mulch with organic matter. The crop should be ready for harvest from mid-autumn.

Parsnip cultivars include the old and well known 'Student' and 'Tender and True', the small 'Alba' and 'New White Skin'.

Parsnip 'New White Skin'

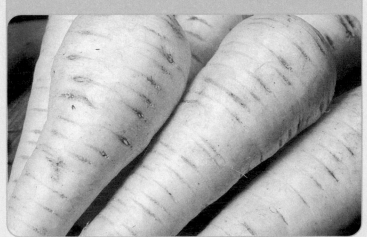

Carrot & Tomato Families

This is a large group that includes such seemingly diverse vegetables as tomato, potato, carrot, parsnip, swede, turnip and radish.

Parsnip and carrot care

Sow:	Fresh seed from mid- to late spring to ensure good germination, or sow earlier having first warmed the soil for a month or so using horticultural fleece. Sow on a still day as parsnip seeds can easily be blown away.
Crop:	Parsnips take around eight months to reach maturity.
Care:	Lime acid soils; water well during dry periods and do not allow the soil to dry out; rotate crops annually.
Pests and diseases:	Parsnip canker causes rot from the crown, often during dry weather. Remove and burn plants.

Carrots

Although we think of carrots as being orange, there are yellow, purple and white carrots, all of which have been cultivated at one time or another. Carrots are grouped according to their root shape at maturity: Autumn King group are large and late to mature; Berlicum group are also late cropping but with cylindrical roots; Chantenay group have tapered, stump roots, ideal for the summer; Nantes group are large and broad, usually early crop; Amsterdam group have small, cylindrical roots; Paris Market are fast maturing, early cropping.

Mini carrots – sweet and tender

Tomatoes

Tomatoes are excellent annual plants for the 'home grower', as they can be grown outdoors, in pots or under glass with relative ease and occupy comparatively little space. New, compact varieties are small enough to be grown on a windowsill indoors and will still produce a reasonable crop. The key factors in tomato cultivation are feeding and watering, as too much feed or too rich a soil will encourage green growth at the expense of fruit, and too much water will spoil the taste of the crop, making the tomatoes taste bland.

Tomato cultivars include the famous 'Moneymaker', which can be grown indoor and outdoors, 'Green Sausage' which is an unusual and highly decorative tomato suitable for containers that will add interest to salads, and 'Tiny Tim', a very compact form that can be grown on a windowsill.

Tomato Standard 'Ailsa Craig'

Tomato Plum 'Roma'

Tomato care

Sow:	Tomato seeds require a minimum temperature of 16°C (61°F) to germinate. Sow in a warm glasshouse from mid-winter, or in an unheated glasshouse from mid-spring.
Crop:	Harvest fruits by breaking at the joint above the fruit, as they ripen.
Care:	Feed with a balanced liquid feed until plants are established, then change to a high potash fertiliser when flowers appear. Water during dry periods, being careful not to overwater.
Pests and diseases:	Whitefly, aphid and red spider mite can attack plants. Blossom end rot, caused by calcium deficiency associated with inconsistent watering, causes dark flattened patches at the base of the fruit. Fruit can split as a consequence of inconsistent watering.

Legumes

Within this group are the peas – mange tout, sugar snap, etc – and French, broad and runner beans.

Runner beans

Runner beans are half hardy perennials that are grown as annuals due to their lack of frost resistance. Older cultivars could become stringy with age, but modern cultivars do not share this characteristic. Runner beans should be sown in late spring or early summer once the soil has warmed, and although they are usually grown on a support system of canes the main stems can be pinched out when young to form a bushy plant that can be grown without supports. Runner bean cultivars include 'Liberty', the early cropping 'Kelvedon Marvel' and the dwarfing 'Pickwick'.

Runner bean 'Desirée'

Runner bean care

Sow:	From late spring to early summer to ensure a minimum heat of 10°C (18°F).
Crop:	Pick regularly to prevent stringiness and ensure a succession of beans, from mid-summer to mid-autumn.
Care:	Apply a general fertilizer before sowing, mulch after germination and water well to establish bud setting and during dry periods.
Pests and diseases:	Slugs, aphids and red spider mite can attack plants. In wet, warm weather Botrytis may be a problem.

Radishes

Radishes are an easy vegetable to grow, maturing quickly and enjoying lighter soil than most vegetables, which makes them suitable for growing in a bed recently vacated by another crop. There are two main groups, salad and over-wintering radish and mooli (or daikon) radish that are distinct from salad radish in being long and white.

Radishes are cool season crops, ideal for spring, autumn and winter – mooli radish are especially suitable for short, cool days – but they can be grown in warmer weather providing they are shaded by other crops. Radishes need to be harvested as soon as they are ready, as they are prone to going woody if left in for too long.

Radish 'French Breakfast 3'

Brassicas

Brassicas include cabbage, cauliflower, radish, swede and turnip. Like all other vegetable groups, crop rotation is important for brassicas, particularly as they have a number of specific pests and diseases associated with them.

Radish care

Sow:	In fortnightly successions from mid-spring to early autumn. Thin the seedlings out to prevent overcrowding. Sow over-wintering radishes in summer and mooli radish in late summer.
Crop:	Harvest the main crop after eight weeks.
Care:	Lime acid soils and apply a slow-release fertilizer. Do not over water, but water weekly during dry periods.
Pests and diseases:	Cabbage fly, flea beetle and slugs can attack plants.

Growing Fruit

One of the main reasons for growing your own fruit is its superior flavour. A lot of supermarket fruit cultivars are grown for yield rather than flavour, and are then refrigerated for transport and storage, affecting the texture. Older fruit cultivars may not produce huge yields, but they will be packed with flavour and texture, especially when the only transportation is from tree or bush to plate!

Almost every garden will have space to grow some kind of fruit tree or bush, but if you want to grow a reasonable amount of fruit, enough to supplement purchased fruit throughout the season or enable self-sufficiency, a little more space will be required.

Specialist training of fruit trees into espaliers, cordons and fans enables productivity to be increased without the need for lots of space. They can also be trained over arches and pergolas to create an attractive and productive garden feature. All

Growing your own fruit is rewarding and will yield superior flavours

fruit trees and bushes will enjoy an open, sunny site with good air circulation, the latter being important to reduce diseases, specifically fungal diseases.

Planting Fruit Trees

Fruit trees are often best planted in autumn whilst the soil is still warm, when they should be planted as containerized specimens. Prepare the soil thoroughly with well rotted manure and apply a balanced, slow release fertilizer before planting.

Rootstocks Fruit trees, especially apple varieties, can be grafted onto rootstocks that display distinct characteristics such as compact or dwarf growth that are ideal for growing fruit in a smaller garden, so make sure that you are buying a tree that has been grafted onto the right kind of rootstock for you, at the point of purchase. Commonly used rootstocks for apples include the dwarfing M27, the poor soil tolerant MM106 and the mid-sized M26. Fruit tree suppliers will be able to advise you on the best stock for your requirements.

Pollination Fruit trees rely on insect pollinators to ensure successful pollination and fruit setting, so plant more than one fruit tree or bush – in the case of apples usually three different varieties are needed – and also consider planting spring flowering trees, shrubs and perennials to attract as many pollinating insects to the garden as possible.

Pruning & Training Fruit Trees

Fruit trees can be grown in a variety of different ways according to the type of fruit and the space available. The majority of fruit trees can be manipulated, through pruning and training, to occupy minimal space and produce more bountiful crops. The development of dwarfing rootstocks further enhances the opportunity to grow productive fruit in limited space.

Over the years a variety of different ways of training fruit trees have been developed, each with its own particular set of advantages and disadvantages. The methods which you choose to use will be largely guided by the space you have available, the quantity and diversity of fruit varieties you wish to grow, physical features in your garden such as walls and fences that might be suitable for plants to grow against, and of course the time you want to spend growing and tending your fruit trees.

Espalier training

This combines beauty and productivity in an easy-to-manage form, and is most suitable for apples and pears. Espaliers involve training the lateral growths of the fruit tree horizontally from the main stem, and then creating a spur system through pruning.

Preparing the support To achieve this, a system of horizontal wires should be fixed to stout posts driven into the ground at 2–2.5m (6½–8ft) spaces. Alternatively the wires can be fixed to a wall or fence using vine eyes and tensioners. The wires need to be tensioned to ensure that they do not sag under the weight of the branches and fruit, and should be evenly spaced at around 40cm (16in).

Planting the tree A young fruit tree with a strong main stem and a few good side shoots should be planted in well prepared ground immediately in front of one of the posts, ensuring that the best lateral growth are parallel with the wires. After planting, select the best side shoots to train in and prune off any unwanted growth.

Training and pruning As the side shoots develop, they should be tied with twine to lengths of bamboo cane, which in turn

The rootstock grafting point on an apple tree

should be tied to the wires, so that the whole is horizontal. The significance of the bamboo cane is that it enables the growth to be tied in frequently and helps to keep the growth straight, without the stems zig-zagging back and forth from the wire. Any buds that form in between the main lateral shoots should be rubbed off to ensure that

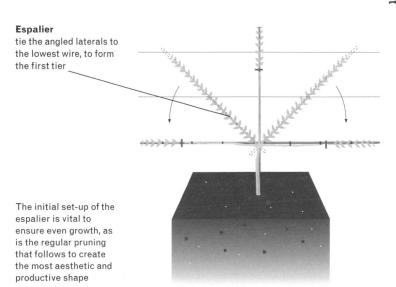

Espalier
tie the angled laterals to the lowest wire, to form the first tier

The initial set-up of the espalier is vital to ensure even growth, as is the regular pruning that follows to create the most aesthetic and productive shape

all of the plant's energy is put into forming growth, flower and fruit on the main stems.

During winter the lateral shoots can be pruned using the spur pruning technique: cutting back the growth from the lateral shoots to within two to three buds.

There are a number of derivatives of espalier training, including 'pitchforks' and 'toasting forks', where short vertical stems are trained from the lateral shoots. Low growing espaliers are often referred to as 'stepovers' and make great edge plants for paths.

Fan training

This is particularly suited to fruit trees that require a warm location to ripen well, and is best carried out by fixing wires (as per Espalier training) to a sunny wall. Apricots, peaches and nectarines are amongst the fruit trees most commonly grown as fan trained specimens. As with Espalier training, use twine and bamboo canes to train the lateral stems, in this case into a

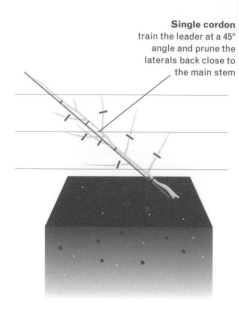

Single cordon
train the leader at a 45° angle and prune the laterals back close to the main stem

Cordons are a good device for a small fruit garden, as the training involved means that cordoned trees end up taking up very little space

fan shape rather than horizontally. Spur prune as per espaliers.

Cordons

These offer the opportunity to grow a wide variety of fruit – usually apples – in a very limited space, as cordons are narrow and upright and can be planted close together. It involves selecting a young tree with few side shoots and planting it at a 60 degree angle to the soil, fixed to a stout post. As the side shoots develop, the strongest should be retained and the rest rubbed or pruned out. These are then spur pruned in winter. Although this method does not produce fruit in quantity it is excellent for ensuring a succession of fruit, as varieties can be planted that fruit at different times through the season.

Standard trees

Standards are those that are allowed to form a more natural 'tree-like' shape with varying degrees of pruning. Apples and pears can be grown in this way, although in both instances spur pruning is usually employed to retain an open, goblet shaped tree. Plums and damsons are best left to

TIP

Most fruit trees suffer from pests and diseases, and consequently can end up looking a real mess for much of the year. However, as long as an appropriate pruning regime is employed they will maintain their vigour and consequently their productivity, so although they may look unsightly they will continue to produce plenty of fruit.

Fan
tie two main laterals on to angled canes, then the following summer select four strong shoots to produce the basic shape

Fan training works best with soft fruits such as peaches and nectarines. The objective is to create a shape like a fan rather than a horizontal orientation

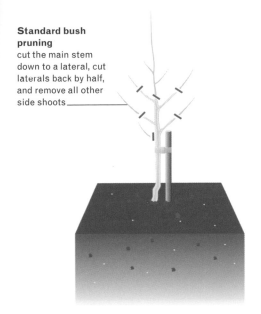

Standard bush pruning
cut the main stem down to a lateral, cut laterals back by half, and remove all other side shoots _____

Regular pruning of standards is essential to ensure the lasting productivity of the tree

achieve their natural form, whilst mulberries can be grown as standards but usually need pollarding every few years to remove unproductive twiggy growth.

Bushes and low standards apply to the more compact, shrubby fruit that require little pruning apart from formative work after planting. Greengages and quinces are usually grown as bushes or low standards.

Pruning & Training Soft Fruits

As with fruit trees, most soft fruits require a regular pruning regime to ensure good cropping, and this can sometimes involve pruning more than once during a growing season.

Raspberries Although there are specific summer and autumn fruiting varieties it is possible to manipulate fruiting by pruning to produce fruit at different times of the year. For summer fruiting, all the old fruiting canes and dead growth should be removed in autumn, and new, young canes tied in at

12cm (5in) spaces. Autumn fruiting varieties should be cut down to the ground in late winter, and new canes thinned out in spring.

Blackberries produce canes that can fruit for more than one year, but new growth usually produces fruit in greater quantity and quality, so the old and dead wood should be cut out in winter and all new canes tied in.

Gooseberries are best grown as a goblet shaped bush and then spur pruned hard back in late winter. They can also be trained vertically as cordons, or given formative pruning and grown as a low standard.

Redcurrants and whitecurrants can be trained and pruned as bushes, espaliers, cordons or fans.

Blackcurrants are pruned back annually to the ground. A third or so of the stems should have all of the shoots removed to ground level.

Dessert grapes To ensure a good crop, a system of wires set at 50cm (20in) spaces should be installed either in a glasshouse or over a pergola. The vine should be hard pruned after planting with the main shoots reduced to four or five in number.

Regular pruning will help ensure higher yields of fruit

An Introduction to Fruit

Growing fresh fruit in your garden may seem ambitious, particularly if your garden is small, but most are large enough to accommodate at least some fruit, especially if space saving training techniques are used.

Orchard fruit

With the availability of modern dwarfing rootstocks comes the opportunity to grow orchard fruit in even the smallest garden.

Apple care

Plant:	In autumn (containerized/container grown) or winter to early spring (bare root). Do not plant near to potatoes as this can encourage potato blight.
Care:	Mulch with organic matter in spring and feed by spraying with a liquid seaweed solution each month. Thin out the fruit in summer to encourage good cropping.
Harvest:	As fruits ripen, keeping the best, least spoiled fruits for storing.
Prune:	In winter and remove any decaying fruits.

Apples – dessert and culinary

Apples have been in cultivation for centuries, and although the oldest varieties are no longer available in commerce, their descendents are still with us. Older varieties tend to have superb flavour and texture but can be prone to disease and rarely produce high yields; however, this should not be too much of a consideration for many gardeners. Select apple varieties that will crop in succession from early autumn to mid-winter, to ensure a regular supply of fruit.

Among the best varieties – based on taste rather than yield, disease resistance or ease of cultivation – are: Ribston Pippin, Granny Smith, Spartan and Discovery.

Apple 'Fiesta'

Pears – dessert and culinary

As with apples, pears have a long established history in cultivation that dates back centuries. Between the 1600s, when pear varieties were in single figures, and the mid-1800s, more than eight hundred different varieties were raised. The pears that are commonly grown today are usually dessert pears, as these can be eaten raw or cooked, whereas culinary pears are only suitable for cooking.

The best varieties grown today include the widely grown Conference, Bartlett, Improved Fertility and Doyenne du Comice.

Pear 'Conference'

Pear care

Plant: In autumn (containerized/container grown) or winter to early spring (bare root) in rich, well drained soil.
Care: Mulch with organic matter in spring and feed by spraying with a liquid seaweed solution monthly. Protect flowers and buds with horticultural fleece during frosty weather. Thin out the fruit in summer to encourage good cropping.
Harvest: As fruits ripen in autumn.
Prune: In winter and apply plenty of composted organic matter.

Plum care

Plant: In autumn (containerized/ container grown) or winter to early spring (bare root).
Care: Mulch with organic matter in spring and feed by spraying with a liquid seaweed solution, protect the flowers with fleece and carry out any pruning required.
Harvest: As fruits ripen, remove any decaying fruit. Protect buds from birds during winter by covering with netting or fleece.

Plums

Plums have been grown at least since Roman times and are believed to have been developed from the wild *Prunus cerasifera* and *Prunus spinosa*. Today, there are varieties that have been bred for conditions as varied as the warmth of California to the cool of Northern Europe. Best grown on rich, moist soils, plums will not tolerate really wet, cold soils – something they share with cherries and other fruiting prunus.

Plums are suitable for growing under glass, particularly as the blossom is susceptible to spring frosts, and are best grown in large pots that can be put outdoors during summer. Popular varieties include the culinary plum 'Czar', which has blossom that is frost resistant, as well as self fertile, the well known old favourite 'Victoria', with its delicious, yellow fleshed fruit, and the late cropping 'Marjorie's Seedling'.

Plum 'Victoria'

Peaches

For many people, the idea that peaches can be grown in comparatively cool climates is difficult to imagine, but peaches originated in China and are grown in regions where there are cool, even very cold, winters. Peaches need this cold winter dormancy period to 'rest', even if they are being grown in a glasshouse, and without it they will fail. They also require plenty of organic matter applied annually as a mulch, to help maintain nutrient and moisture levels, but they will not tolerate waterlogging.

Reliable varieties include Peregrine, Royal George and Rochester.

Peach 'Peregrine'

Peach care

Plant: In autumn (containerized/container grown) or winter to early spring (bare root), in rich, moist but well drained soil.

Care: Mulch with organic matter in spring and feed by spraying with a liquid seaweed solution monthly. Protect blossom from frost, hand pollinate. Thin out the fruit in summer to prevent branches from breaking and protect fruits from wasps and birds with cotton or fleece.

Harvest: As fruits ripen.

Prune: Hard back in winter and remove any remaining decaying fruits.

Soft Fruit

Soft fruits tend to be a favourite food of many birds, so protection is often needed to prevent the entire crop being eaten. This can be achieved through constructing a fruit cage, consisting of a frame made from metal or wood with netting stretched over the top and sides and a removable or hinged door at one end. There are many companies that supply and erect fruit cages. Alternatively, make a wigwam out of old bamboo canes.

All soft fruit will respond well to a really good mulch of well rotted organic matter during winter or early spring.

Redcurrants

Redcurrants are long lived shrubs that enjoy a rich, cool soil and can be grown with success in partial shade. Tough and resilient, they can withstand incorrect pruning and are often one of the last of the shrubby fruiting plants to die off in an abandoned fruit garden. The crop, however, is a favourite food source for birds and needs protecting with netting if it is not to be decimated.

Popular varieties are Wilson's Longbunch and Raby Castle.

Redcurrant 'Jonkeer van Tets'

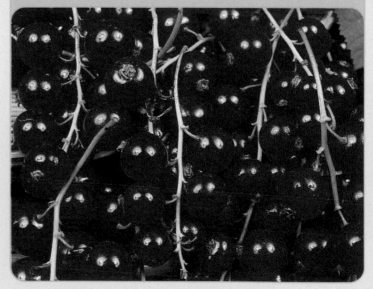

Redcurrant care

Plant: In autumn (containerized/container grown) or winter (bare root) in cool, fertile soil in partial shade or sun.

Care: Mulch heavily with organic matter in spring and feed by spraying with a liquid seaweed solution monthly. Take cuttings in autumn.

Harvest: As fruits ripen.

Prune: In mid-summer after harvest and again in winter.

Raspberry care

Plant: In autumn (containerized/container grown) or winter to early spring (bare root) in cool moist soil.

Care: Mulch heavily with organic matter in spring and feed by spraying with a liquid seaweed solution monthly. Protect fruits during summer and autumn. Tie in the canes during summer. Propagate by tip layering in spring.

Harvest: As fruits ripen during late summer/autumn.

Prune: To the ground in winter, mulch heavily.

Dessert grape care

Plant: In autumn (containerized/container grown).

Care: Mulch with organic matter in spring and feed by spraying with a liquid seaweed solution monthly. Thin out the grape bunches in summer to encourage good cropping and nip out the ends of the shoots.

Harvest: As fruits ripen, provide protection for outdoor grapes.

Prune: Hard in winter.

Raspberries

Raspberries enjoy cool conditions, making them ideal for colder areas and for growing in partial shade, with plenty of organic matter used to enrich the soil. Raspberry varieties are either summer or autumn cropping, ensuring a good spread of fruit for harvesting which is important as raspberries do not keep well once picked. Because of this they are often made into preserves and jams.

There are numerous varieties of raspberries available.

Raspberry 'Driscolls'

Dessert grapes

To ensure good fruiting, dessert grapes are best grown under glass, with the vine planted outside the greenhouse and a hole made in the wall through which the vine is trained, into the greenhouse and onto a system of wires. As these are productive plants that also have ornamental value they can, and often are, grown outdoors over pergolas and arches.

Reliable varieties under glass include the excellent Muscat Hamburg, with firm, sweet tasting grapes, and the old and established 'Black Hamburg' with large grapes in big bunches. Outdoors, try the golden fruited 'Golden Chasselas' or spicy 'Siegerrebe'. Both will benefit from being trained on a warm, sunny wall.

Grape 'Muscat of Alexandria'

Herbs

If you enjoy cooking at home then having a ready supply of fresh herbs is a real boon, as the flavour they bring to food is quite unlike that of dried herbs. Best of all, herbs do not huge amounts of space and can be readily grown in containers, windowsills, even hanging baskets, and are easy to incorporate into an ornamental garden setting.

Herbs have a long history of cultivation, having been grown for their curative qualities as much as their culinary value.

Today, herbs are mainly grown for culinary and aromatic reasons, but they still retain their status as hugely practical and productive plants, with ornamental value to boot.

Where to grow herbs

The majority of herbs originate from the Mediterranean, and thrive in hot, dry and sunny conditions, with sharply drained soil. If you are planning a herb garden from scratch, choose a location in your garden that has sun for most if not all of the day. If space is at a premium, grow herbs in containers or windowboxes, or use herbs such as oregano and thyme as edging for a gravel, brick or stone path, or in a patio.

Culinary and salad herbs

Culinary herbs are best grown as close as possible to the kitchen, where the convenience of having them close to hand will soon be

Medicinal herbs

Comfrey (*Symphytum officinale*)
English Marigold (*Calendula officinalis*)
Feverfew (*Tanacetum parthenium*)
Flag Iris (*Iris versicolor*)
Houseleek (*Sempervivum tectorum*)
Lady's Mantle (*Alchemilla mollis*)
Meadowsweet (*Filipendula ulmaria*)
Peppermint (*Mentha* x *piperita*)

Pots and containers are ideal for growing herbs

appreciated. Full sun is important as it will enhance the flavour of the herbs, many of which are packed with oils that become more prominent in a sunny spot.

Medicinal herbs

Medicinal herbs are still widely used to make infusions, cosmetic compounds and natural remedies. Many of these can be grown at home, but it is essential that if you intend to use medicinal herbs you consult a herbal practitioner or your family doctor, as some are potentially harmful if taken in large doses or incorrectly prepared.

Many medicinal herbs are also common garden plants, some of which you may already have in your own garden. Furthermore, some of the salad and culinary herbs also have medicinal properties.

Greenhouse Gardening

A greenhouse in your garden opens up a wide range of opportunities for growing and propagating plants, enabling you to experience ever broader aspects of gardening. The controlled environment of a greenhouse allows you to grow more exotic or specialist plants. Alpines, cacti and succulents will benefit from protection from wet winter conditions, and will require no extra heating. However, if you are adventurous, and do not mind the fuel bills entailed with keeping a hot house, then you can experiment with growing many tropical species and create ornamental displays of tender plants. Even if creating a rainforest under glass does not appeal, a greenhouse will still enable you to grow more exotic plants in the garden at large as it provides useful shelter for over-wintering half-hardy perennials, ready to plant out in spring after the winter frosts have passed.

A greenhouse can also help to increase the productive capacity of your garden. If you enjoy growing your own food a greenhouse will allow you to cultivate crops that benefit from warmer conditions, and to increase cropping seasons by starting off seedlings early and growing out-of-season vegetables. Greenhouses also provide the perfect environment for exploring the art of propagation to increase your stock of plants and prepare for spring and summer bedding. The advantages are many, and the knowledge that can be gained through using one is immense. Greenhouses are great for gardeners of all ages and are invaluable for introducing children to the growth and also the care of plants.

Types of Greenhouse

There are many styles and sizes of greenhouse available, and it is really a case of choosing the one that suits your needs best, by considering what you want to grow, how much space you need and how much space in your garden you want to give up to a greenhouse.

Freestanding

Freestanding greenhouses are traditionally straight sided with a pitched roof and either fully glazed or with a brick or timber base extending around 1m (3ft) from the ground. They can be of timber, alloy, steel, cast iron or occasionally UPVC construction. They all have similar qualities as far as growing is concerned: good light penetration and ventilation being key requirements for growing plants in greenhouses.

There are a number of variations to the traditional straight-sided house.

Dutch light greenhouses are usually made of alloy, fully glazed with a pitched roof and sides that gently flare out to the base. In commercial horticulture, such houses are often mounted on rails so that they can be manoeuvred over crops.

Curvilinear houses are made from alloy, fully glazed and are primarily used by commercial growers or very enthusiastic amateurs.

Geodesic glasshouses are based on Buckminster Fuller's invention, the geodesic dome, and are usually of alloy construction. They make excellent display houses and are great to look at, but can be hard to kit out with benching owing to their unusual shape.

Lean-tos

Lean-to greenhouses are good in smaller spaces as they are constructed against an existing wall, usually the wall of a house. In some instances they double up as a conservatory. The one major disadvantage of lean-to houses is that their positioning will be dictated by the available wall space, and if this is, for example, on the shaded side of the house, then it will restrict the plants that can be grown to shade tolerant plants such as ferns.

Polythene

Polythene tunnels offer a cost effective way of protecting crops, and are made from heavy grade polythene stretched over a framework of tubular steel hoops. From a growing perspective they are not dissimilar to greenhouses, although light levels are lower due to the type of covering material, and ventilation can be problematical.

There are designs of greenhouse to suit every size and style of garden

Greenhouse Construction & Siting

Greenhouses tend to be tucked away in the corner of the garden, as if something of an embarrassment. But by choosing an attractive greenhouse in the first place, there is no need for it to be relegated to a dingy corner where the growing conditions are likely to be far from ideal. Furthermore, it is possible to incorporate a greenhouse as part of the design of a garden so that it becomes an ornamental feature in its own right; a focal point at the end of a path or pergola, or surrounded by a patio with tables, chairs and a barbecue, perhaps.

Choose materials that have aesthetic qualities and your greenhouse need not be an eyesore

Construction materials

Greenhouses are constructed from a variety of materials and the type you choose will depend on aesthetic considerations and those relating to maintenance. For example, an alloy greenhouse will require little maintenance but may be less aesthetically pleasing than one made of white painted wood, which will require quite considerable maintenance over the years. Recently a number of manufacturers have begun to produce very attractive greenhouses from cast alloy that looks like traditional cast iron, and from western red cedar, a resinous wood with an attractive reddish brown

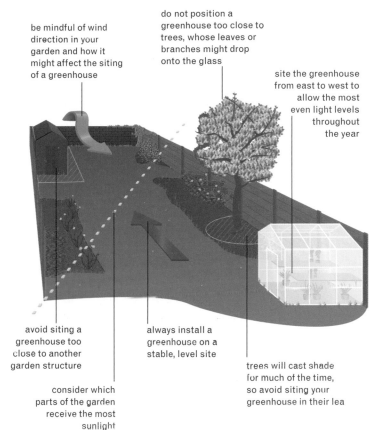

be mindful of wind direction in your garden and how it might affect the siting of a greenhouse

do not position a greenhouse too close to trees, whose leaves or branches might drop onto the glass

site the greenhouse from east to west to allow the most even light levels throughout the year

avoid siting a greenhouse too close to another garden structure

consider which parts of the garden receive the most sunlight

always install a greenhouse on a stable, level site

trees will cast shade for much of the time, so avoid siting your greenhouse in their lea

colour that needs neither treating with preservative nor painting.

Where to site

The most important considerations from the growing perspective are shelter from strong winds and good light levels. The latter point is especially important for the healthy growth of plants and for over-wintering, and care should be taken to make sure that what seems a light, open location in summer is not completely shaded out by trees or buildings in the winter months.

> **TIP**
>
> Another consideration for whether you opt for a house that is glazed to the ground or has a brick, block or timber base is safety. A greenhouse that is glazed to the floor may be less safe for small children and pets that might run into the glass, than one with a solid base.

Fitting Out a Greenhouse

Of course a greenhouse is not much use with nothing in it, and fitting out the greenhouse to suit your growing needs is vital. If, for example, you want nothing more than to grow tomatoes in grow bags, then you will not need staging or benches. But if your passion is for Auriculas, then you will certainly want staging, and probably lots of it! Typically, a well kitted greenhouse will include the following:

Ventilation and humidity

Vents usually come fitted as standard to greenhouses, and indeed should be included

Staging in the greenhouse brings plants up to eye level, making them easier to work with

Some greenhouses feature adjustable glass slats as part of their system of ventilation

in the specification. How many vents will depend on the size of the greenhouse, but as a guide a 4 x 2m (13 x 7ft) greenhouse should have at least two vents. These can be roof mounted, side mounted or louvre ventilators. Ideally these vents will be automated, and although it is possible to fit electronically operated vents, a simple hydraulic vent which is triggered by temperature changes is fine. Good ventilation is essential in a greenhouse if plants are not to suffer from excessive humidity and resultant moulds and mildews. Humidifiers can be purchased from many outlets and help to keep humidity levels constant, in conjunction with venting to prevent excessive humidity. The right level of humidity in a glasshouse will help with propagation and growing, but there is no

What's the use of a greenhouse?

Greenhouses offer the following advantages to the gardener:

- A space to propagate plants. Greenhouses are undoubtedly the best place to propagate and grow on plants, particularly if the greenhouse is equipped with heating.
- A place to over-winter tender plants. Containers and baskets can be brought into the greenhouse for winter protection, as can 'plunged' plants (half hardy perennial plants, trees or shrubs that are bedded out in a border for the summer months) and exotics such as palms and cacti.
- A place to grow winter flowering or fruiting plants that produce flowers or fruit in winter, for example citrus trees that can crop into winter but would not be hardy if left outdoors in cooler climes.
- A productive space for vegetables needing protection, such as tomatoes and cucumbers.
- A place to force plants. Forcing is an old technique used to encourage plants into growth or flower earlier in the season than would be normal. For example, canna lilies are popular sub-tropical plants that are usually bedded out after the risk of late frosts has passed, but by increasing the temperature progressively in the greenhouse they can be forced into growth and be bedded out at a more mature stage, reaching flowering earlier than they would otherwise.
- A space for specialist plants such as alpines, half hardy ferns and so on.

scientific level at which this should be set, rather it is by observation and trial and error that you will establish your requirements.

Staging and benching

Depending entirely on how you want to use the greenhouse these can be made from wooden slats or purpose-built alloy benches.

Irrigation

Automatic watering can save time and ensure that plants are being regularly watered, even when you are away. Automated systems use a simple timer system operated by a microchip, and are available from many manufacturers.

Heating and insulation

Unheated greenhouses are perfectly usable for many plants, but having some heating – if only enough to keep the house frost free – will dramatically increase the range of plants you can grow and the comfort in which you can work. Ensure that the heater you buy is specifically for greenhouse use. To help retain heat and maintain temperatures, even in an unheated house, insulating plastic – commonly known as bubble wrap – can be fitted to the glazing of the greenhouse.

Install an automatic watering system to make watering less of a chore

Maintaining a greenhouse

A greenhouse is quite an investment, and well worth taking a little time and trouble over to keep it in its best condition. Basic maintenance includes:

- Clearing gutters at regular intervals. If the gutters get blocked the storm water can run down into the greenhouse, causing structural problems and affecting growing conditions in the house itself.
- Maintaining wood framed greenhouses, either by painting with wood preservative treatment or paint.
- Replacing broken or chipped glass which can shatter in times of temperature change.
- Checking heating and ventilation systems regularly to ensure they work when you need them to.

Clear greenhouse gutters regularly

TIP

Greenhouse pests can cause problems quite early in the season, as the heat and protection in a greenhouse makes conditions ideal. Good hygiene is essential in controlling pests, removing dead leaves and plants, and clearing away the debris that pests can hide in. A thorough clean in mid-winter will really help, to the point of scrubbing between the glazing bars of the greenhouse.

A Year in the Greenhouse

Like any other part of the garden, a greenhouse requires different levels of maintenance and attention at different times of the year. This seasonal guide is not comprehensive, but covers all the essential jobs that need undertaking in the greenhouse as the seasons change. Basic advice on plant care is also provided.

Bubble wrap makes ideal insulation for greenhouses and should be replaced every winter

Winter

Early winter
- Replace insulating materials
- Remove all dead and diseased or damaged plants, leaves and debris

Mid-winter
- Check over the heating equipment, heating and ventilation in the house. Heating should be set at a level that keeps the house frost free, typically 4.5°C–5°C (40–41°F).
- Water 'resting' plants sparingly, flowering plants regularly.
- Keep humidity levels low to discourage moulds.
- Propagate short day flowering plants such as chysanthemums.
- Sow Canna, Pelargonium and Fuchsia.

Late winter
- Maintain the minimum temperature in the greenhouse but ventilate during the day.
- Step up watering levels.
- Sow seed of plants that require long germination periods and those that need to be grown on for some time before planting out such as Salvia, sweet pea (Lathyrus), Begonia.
- Plant out tomato plants.
- Sow vegetables for transplanting: brassicas, onions, carrots, parsnips, beetroot.

Spring

Early spring
- Continue to increase watering and maintain humidity, but ventilate the greenhouse thoroughly on sunny days.
- Sow peppers, half hardy annuals, bedding plants.
- At this time of year pests can begin to appear – whitefly, aphid and red spider mite – so introduce biological controls, sticky traps and cultural controls to keep problems at bay.
- Begin re-potting orchids.

Mid-spring
- Continue to increase watering and maintain humidity; ventilate the greenhouse thoroughly on sunny days; maintain frost free night time temperatures.
- Re-pot orchids, pot on potbound plants.
- Sow cucumbers, courgettes, marrows and pumpkins for transplanting outdoors.
- Sow runner beans and dwarf French beans for transplanting outdoors.
- Transplant seedlings into larger pots to give them more growing room.
- Begin to move established half hardy plants and bedding into cold frames (or outdoors during the day, back in the greenhouse at night) to allow them to harden off.

Late spring
- Water regularly including damping down the floor of the glasshouse.
- Paint the outside of the greenhouse with light reflective whitewash to increase shade inside the house.
- Pot on pelargoniums and begonias.
- Pinch out the growing tips of fuchsias to encourage bushy growth.
- Feed plants with a balanced liquid feed.
- Tie in the shoots of tomatoes.
- Plant out tender perennials.

Pot on seedlings in mid-spring to give them more space to develop at the height of the growing season

Summer

Early summer
- Ventilate constantly during the day and on warm evenings.
- Turn off heaters.
- Plant out bedding plants
- Water twice or three times daily as needed, and damp down the floor.
- Feed tomatoes.
- Begin to take semi-ripe cuttings.
- Put over wintering plants outdoors.
- Remove insulating materials

Mid-summer
- Keep watering! Ventilate continuously as required.
- Continue to take semi-ripe cuttings.
- Harvest cucumbers and tomatoes as they ripen.
- Pinch out tomatoes to encourage bushy growth, and cucumber laterals.
- Add additional shading inside the house if needed, using mesh netting.

Late summer
- Continue watering, damping down and ventilating.
- Sow spring flowering annuals.
- Begin to plant in pots winter and spring flowering bulbs such as tulips, hyacinths and daffodils (Narcissus).
- Mulch tomatoes, apply a high potash liquid feed to flowering plants.
- Take Pelargonium cuttings.

Autumn

Early autumn
- Begin to reduce watering and stop damping down, continue to ventilate on warm days.
- Check over heaters to make sure they work, and be aware of night time temperature drops.
- Reduce shading by removing mesh netting.
- Take cuttings from bedding plants and tender perennials
- Bring half hardy plants that have been outdoors for the summer back indoors.
- Remove tomato plants and growing bags to the compost heap
- Pot on spring flowering plants.
- Begin to take hardwood cuttings.

Mid-autumn
- Keep the greenhouse frost free by switching on the heating system.
- Further reduce watering, continue ventilating.
- Remove the whitewash shading from the outside of the greenhouse.
- Feed spring flowering plants.
- Clear up any dead or decaying plant matter.
- Take hardwood cuttings.

Late autumn
- Reduce watering and ventilation to a minimum.
- Pot on bedding plants struck as cuttings.
- Sow lettuce for early cropping.

Introduce heaters to the greenhouse with the onset of autumn

Lawns

Lawns can be the making or the breaking of a garden. A really good lawn will set off the plants in the garden beautifully, whilst a patchy, weed ridden one will look a mess and will be difficult to care for. There are a number of different ways to achieve a fine lawn, by improving what you have or starting from scratch, and the route you take will depend on how patient you are and how much money you want to spend. This is important, because a good lawn can take more time and cost than a planted border.

But before we get to that point, consider what you want to get from your lawn and how you use it. If you have young children and pets, then a fine sward (the name used for describing the make-up of the lawn grasses) is likely to be almost impossible, and a hardwearing lawn should be the aim. If you want space for entertaining, then a large area of lawn might be the way to go, but equally a paved area or gravel could be the answer. Whatever you do, make your lawn no bigger than the size you really need. A really big lawn can be a burden in terms of maintenance and if all you need is the space for a table and a couple of chairs, you would be well advised to reduce the size of the lawn — you will then have much more space for plants!

Creating a New Lawn

If you do not already own a lawn, or have one that is so poor that only starting over again makes sense, then there are two options – laying turf or growing from seed. In both cases the preparation is the same, so let's deal with that first.

Soil Preparation

The key to successfully establishing any new lawn is in the preparation, so spend as much time as possible getting it right. Whether you are laying turf or sowing seed, start by digging over or rotavating the site, removing any plant material, roots, weeds and large stones. Use a rake to further break down the soil and remove

medium-sized stones, raking in two or three different directions. At this stage you should also try to even out any crests or hollows by moving the soil around with the rake, or 'skimming and filling' with a shovel, taking the soil from the crests to fill in the hollows. Once the soil is level and raked to a fine tilth, you need to tread the site by walking back and forth using 'pigeon steps' or on larger sites by using a roller, in order to help settle the soil – but not compact it. Finally, rake the soil over again to loosen the surface.

Laying Turf

Using turf is the quickest way to establish a new lawn, as you will get almost instant results. Providing the turf is laid correctly

Choosing quality turf

Turf should be weed free, moist but not wet (and definitely not dry) and freshly cut at around 7–12 cm (3–5in) thick. Cut too thinly, the turf will have an inadequate root system and will be prone to drying, whilst if it is too thick it will be hard work to lay and will take ages to root into the soil. Check the turf while it is still on the delivery lorry, and reject it if it is of poor quality.

and given plenty of aftercare, the lawn will root and settle quickly. Turfing can be done at any time of the year, unlike sowing from seed, as long as you can provide regular watering as the turf establishes. The disadvantages with turfing are the initial cost and subsequent care, as newly laid turf needs lots of water during dry periods for the first season of growth.

Turf or grass seed? The choice is yours, depending on your requirements

Step-by-step turf laying

1 – When laying turf, start at the far end of the site and work backwards; you will then not be walking over freshly laid turf. Lay turf using what bricklayers call 'stretcher bond', – the staggered method used for laying bricks. This ensures that the edges of turf – the bit most prone to dry out – don't all end up in a row.

2 – When butting up two rolls of turf, lay one slightly over the edge of the next, and then cut through both using a sharp, long bladed knife such as a carving knife. This will ensure the two edges 'key in' perfectly.

3 – Use a board to spread your weight over laid turf and to help bed the turf in.

4 – Use a half moon edging iron to cut around border edges or features such as trees. On completion, irrigate the lawn extensively, ideally for around 10 minutes per square metre, and continue irrigating daily for the first two weeks and in dry weather thereafter for the rest of the season. The lawn will have rooted and should be useable after about a month.

Sowing Grass Seed

Creating a new lawn using grass seed is quick to do and very cheap, but can take up to two months from sowing to achieve a useable lawn. Establishing a lawn from seed is only really possible in spring or autumn.

Step-by-step sowing

1 – Prepare the soil by breaking it up and raking it into an even tilth.

2 – Firm the soil by treading it down with small steps up and down the seeding area.

3 – Rake the soil lightly once more to break it up, ready to receive the grass seed.

4 – Sprinkle grass seed over the seeding bed either by using a drop spreader or by broadcast sowing – throwing the seed across the area by hand.
   Having seeded the area, lightly rake the seed into the soil surface and then irrigate well. The seed will need regular watering as it establishes itself and might require protection from marauding birds.

1

2

3

4

Grass seed and turf mixtures

Grass seed and turf is available in different mixtures for a variety of applications, including hardwearing areas, fine turf and shade tolerant mixtures. Ask your supplier for advice when selecting turf or seed, but as a rough guide ryegrass seed mixes are better for hardwearing lawns.

1

2

3

4

Lawn Maintenance

The steps required to improve an existing lawn involved basic, good maintenance and husbandry. Regular cutting helps, but every spring or autumn (or both for a really bad lawn) the following steps should be taken, which will eventually lead to an excellent, hard wearing lawn.

Scarifying

Using a spring rake, scarify your lawn by raking vigorously to remove the underlying thatch – the build up of dead grass – and thereby improve root growth and the take up of nutrients and water. If you have a weed or clover problem and you want to use a chemical control, this should be done a few days before scarifying.

Scarifying can make the lawn look scruffy when first executed, but it is highly beneficial in the long run

Tining and top-dressing

Next, take a border fork or aerator to compacted or worn areas of turf, digging the tines in as deeply as possible and then wiggling back and forth to improve drainage. A little sandy loam, or pure sand, broadcast over these holes and then worked in with a flat rake or stiff broom will help to boost soil structure and improve the root zone.

Feeding

Finally, give the whole lawn a feed with a preparatory lawn fertilizer. Spring/summer feed is high in nitrogen to encourage growth

Two important points: never carry out turf maintenance in conditions of extreme drought, wet or cold, and always water your lawn well after applying fertilizer.

and greenness, whilst autumn feed in rich in potassium and phosphorus, the nutrients required to improve root growth and hardiness in lawn grasses. Given the rather punishing nature of the procedures above, I find that feeding with autumn fertilizer, applied at half rate, helps the lawn to recover quickly.

Patching up

Ruts, bumps and bald patches of turf can also be dealt with now. Cut around the damaged area with a half moon and then lift the turf with a turfing iron or spade. The resultant bump or dip can then be either

To repair a patch of worn or damaged turf, cut a good piect of turf from another part of the lawn. Check that the turf is level with the surrounding grass and firm it down before watering

levelled or filled before the turf is replaced and firmed in well with a tamper or the back of a shovel.

Alternative Lawns

Increasingly gardeners are reducing the size of their lawn and experimenting with areas of long grass or mini-wildflower meadows. Furthermore, areas of bulbs naturalized in grass or even perennials planted in grass can add a new dimension to a garden and reduce lawn maintenance. You do not need a big garden to try some of these methods: in my last garden I had three mini-meadows that were no bigger than the average dining table. The following methods are all suitable to try – why not give it a go?

Cornfield Annuals

Cornfield annuals are highly attractive flowering 'weeds' that were, historically, found amongst arable crops, but have now declined to the point of becoming locally

As easy as mowing a lawn

Although many people think that mowing a lawn is easy, doing it correctly is actually something of a science. Firstly, it is important to remember that grass is a living thing, not some kind of indestructible carpet that can be used and abused.

Do not cut too short A common mistake made by amateur gardeners is to cut the grass far too short in summer, exposing the meristem of the leaf blade to the hot sun and 'scalping' the grass. This leads to the grass going yellow and dying off and encourages the growth of weeds and moss. So, once you have reduced the height of the grass in spring (to around 6cm/2in or so for the 'average' lawn) keep it at that height and do not be tempted to cut the grass shorter.

Mow often Regular cutting, twice a week ideally, with the mower set at a height that tips the grass and no more will improve the sward by reducing broadleaved weeds that will not be able to withstand the regular cutting back.

Clippings In hot weather, do not collect the clippings but instead let them mulch back into the lawn, which will help to keep moisture in the sward and boost nutrient levels.

extinct. In order to germinate they rely on soil disturbance – as would take place during ploughing in an agricultural scenario. Once established, a sowing of cornfield annuals will become largely self-regenerating, although the relative quantities of plants should be monitored and where one species declines it should be reintroduced by sowing additional seed.

Below is a timetable for the establishment and maintenance of a cornfield annual sowing.

Autumn to early winter:

- Mark out the intended area – it needs to be in full sun – and remove the grass sward either mechanically (either with a motorized turf cutter) or by hand.
- Dig over or rotavate the soil, then rake and roll (or tread) to create a good, even seed bed.

> **TIP**
> Cornfield annuals can be used to provide quick cover and colour when establishing a perennial wildflower meadow, by adding some cornfield annual seed to the overall seed mix.

- Sow with a cornfield annual mix at the recommended rate.
- Germination should take place within one to three months, depending on the prevailing weather conditions.

Mid-summer:

- Flowering period for cornfield annuals. No maintenance required. These cornfield annuals suppress weeds as well as sheltering the wild flower seedlings.

Late summer:

- Cut the entire sowing using a brushcutter with a metal blade, a scythe or a rotary mower on a high setting without the collection box.
- After one week (in dry conditions), turn the cuttings using a rake. This will help to shed and disperse any seed. If the weather is wet, leave the cuttings for a little while longer and turn them twice if needs be.
- After a further two days to one week, collect the cuttings and put them on the compost heap.

Early autumn:

- Lightly rotavate or dig over the area, then rake and roll (or tread).
- Top up any species that have declined with brought-in seed.

If your cornfield annual meadow is struggling to compete with coarse grasses, blend in some yellow rattle seeds to the mix, or over-sow with yellow rattle in the autumn.

Cornfield annuals bring an old-fashioned country feel to a garden

Perennial Wildflower Meadows

Perennial wildflower meadows differ from cornfield annuals in that they are truly perennial – that is, they live for more than one season – and do not require soil disturbance to ensure seed germination. Less spectacular than cornfield annuals, and containing many species of wild grasses along with flowering plants, perennial wildflower meadows are hugely significant for wildlife, especially invertebrates such as butterflies and moths. Perennial wildflowers are largely endemic and would traditionally be found in full sun as a component of unimproved hay meadows, which are managed for a summer hay crop and then grazed during autumn/winter. They prefer nutrient deficient soils, indeed low nutrient levels are important if the incursion of 'rank herbs' – nettles, dock and the like – is to be prevented. Soil can be 'un-improved' by removing the top few centimetres (inches) of soil, or by mixing sub-soil with the topsoil. There are a number of different establishment methods, and the route taken

Rhinanthus minor

Using yellow (hay) rattle

Yellow Rattle (*Rhinanthus minor*), also known as Hay Rattle, is an annual plant of old hay meadows, with yellow flowers and distinctive seed pods that rattle when dry, hence the common names. Its importance in establishing meadows is as a suppressor of grasses, which in early years can overwhelm flowering plants. *R. minor* is semi-parasitic, and germinates with the grasses and in doing so reduces their vigour, leaving the sward open and better suited to wildflowers.

If *R. minor* is being used, it should be included in the main sowing in autumn. To ensure the colony survives over two to three years, mowing during autumn/winter (to simulate grazing) should be suspended after mid- to late autumn, to ensure that germinating plants are not 'mown off'.

will depend on the desired rate of establishment. Subsequent maintenance is the same in all instances.

Method 1: Establishment from plugs

This method is suitable only for smaller areas, or when rapid establishment is not an issue.

Autumn to early winter:
- Mark out squares of a regular size from 1 x 1m (3 x 3ft) up to 4 x 4m (13 x 13ft), and strip away the grass and topsoil to a depth of 20–30cm (8–12in), leaving the squares somewhat lower than the surrounding soil. Plant up these squares with wildflower plugs, which should establish within twelve months.

A wildflower meadow will act as a magnet for wildlife in your garden, whatever its size

Method 2, establishment from introduced seed

Autumn to early winter:
- Strip away the grass and topsoil to a depth of 20–30cm (8–12in). Lightly rotavate, rake and roll or tread to create a good seed bed.
- Sow with a perennial wildflower mixture suitable for your soil type – wildflower seed suppliers provide a range of mixes designed for different soils.

Early spring:
• Spot treat any emerging rank herbs – dock, nettle, creeping thistle – with glyphosate or dig them out using a trowel. If identification is a problem, this can be carried out later in the year when the plants are easier to spot.

Year 2 and on-going maintenance
Mid- to late summer:
• Cut using a brushcutter with a metal blade, a scythe or a rotary mower on a high setting without the collection box. Turn the clippings with a rake after a week or so, then rake up and remove to the compost heap.

Mid- to late autumn:
• Using a mower with collector, mow the meadow area two or three times, depending on the level of growth. This is to simulate animal grazing (which reduces grass vigour) which traditionally would have taken place on hay meadows, so it is essential that the clippings are collected and removed. Failure to do so will boost the nutrient levels in the meadow and encourage rank herbs at the expense of wildflowers and grasses.

Perennials Naturalized in Grass

This is a fairly new area of gardening and still quite experimental, but in essence involves the use of cultivated plants – bulbs, grasses and flowering perennials – to create an ornamental meadow, which is maintained in the same way as a perennial meadow (see above).

The autumn before planting, cut the grass area very short, to the point of being scalped, and you can sow with yellow rattle to further reduce the vigour of the grasses. Plant the perennials the following spring or

Perennials for naturalizing

Suitable plants, many of which originate from the North American prairies, include:

Allium 'Globemaster'
Allium sphaerocephalum
Anthericum lilliago
Borago officinalis
Camassia cusikii
Deschampsia cespitosa
Echinacea purpurea
Lythrum salicaria
Molinia caerulea
Panicum virgatum
Rudbeckia hirta
Sanguisorba canadensis
Silphium laciniatum

For how to naturalize bulbs in grass, see page 69.

Rudbeckia planted in grass can be used to apply a variety of different visual effects in the garden

in autumn, along with spring flowering bulbs. When planting, remove a square of turf twice as large as the plant pot size to reduce competition and help the plant to get going, and arrange the plants as per bulbs in grass to get a natural, drifting effect.

Alternative Lawns

Container Gardening

Planting in containers offers great scope for growing different plants, as the conditions in a container are easier to manipulate than those for an entire garden. For example, containers can be moved indoors or wrapped up in winter, and the growing medium can be manipulated more readily. Containers can be used as a means of growing plants that we would love to have in our gardens but that our soil or climate preclude – such as Rhododendron, Pieris and Camellia which all require ericaceous compost – but also as a means of maintaining seasonality through the use of bedding plants.

Containers can offer the potential to experiment with different plants and to fill with flowers and foliage parts of the garden where 'planted' plants will not grow. Furthermore, there is great potential in the range of containers now available, well beyond the orange-peel faux terracotta that for so long was the only alternative to the real thing.

Windowboxes can also be planted with an interesting range of plants, and herbs or vegetables can be especially handy when planted in a windowbox outside the kitchen.

What to Plant

Conventional container and windowbox planting usually focuses on fairly standard annual plants such as Impatiens, bedding Lobelia, Verbena, Petunia and Argyranthemum, but why not try something a little more daring...?

Making a bold statement

Bold architectural plants are excellent subjects for containers, and there is nothing new in planting pots with topiary, and in particular box (*Buxus sempervirens*) and bay (*Laurus nobilis*). But there are other, equally structural plants that are well worth trying as an alternative. *Viburnum tinus* cultivars make superb container plants, producing an abundance of flowers during late winter and early spring, and responding well to formative pruning (see page 78), which should be carried out during mid-summer. Shady corners can be illuminated with variegated evergreens such as *Elaeagnus* x *ebbingei* 'Maculata' and 'Gilt Edge'.

Grasses

Ornamental grasses are highly effective in containers, particularly the late flowering *Panicum virgatum* 'Rubrum', with its bluish

This colourful, upright *Carex buchananii* is shown to its full advantage in a galvanized metal pot

green leaves stained with red. *Calamagrostis* 'Karl Foerster' creates a superb vertical accent, its purplish inflorescences gradually turning to the colour of straw, and remaining attractive all through winter.

Given that the main strength of ornamental grasses is their foliage, they can be used to combine and contrast with the colour and form of the container in which they are planted. For example, the powder blue *Elymus magellenicus* is stunning when planted against galvanised zinc or gunmetal grey, while the golden variegated, shade tolerant *Hakonechloa macra* 'Aureola' complements everything from terracotta to wooden half-barrels. There are many other equally exotic grasses to choose from.

Planting the perfect container

Taking a little time to plant your containers correctly will save hours of watering come summer time.

Drainage Ensure good drainage by placing crocks in the base of the container. Traditionally these were broken clay pots, but if the container is large and you are seeking to reduce its overall weight then you could use polystyrene packaging as an alternative.

Wetting agent Mix the compost – ideally a loam based one – with a wetting agent. These are granules that expand into jelly when watered, and then release the water to the plants gradually over time. Using these granules can save a great deal of watering time, but remember to use them at the right rate if you want to avoid your plants erupting from the container!

Filling with compost When the container is three-quarters full of compost, set out the plants and then top up around them, ensuring that the finished compost level is at least 5cm (2in) below the rim of the container. This will create a reservoir when watering, whereas filling the container to the brim will cause water to run off.

Winter positioning During winter, place containers with less hardy subjects against the wall of your house, in the 'rain shadow'. This will protect against frost damage.

Exotica

Gardeners have for centuries used containers to display exotic and tender plants during the summer months, but if you do not have a glasshouse or conservatory to overwinter them in this may seem unattainable. However, there are a number of hardy plants that can create the same ambience, without recourse to winter cover. The Fishtail Palm, *Chamaerops humilis*, is compact in growth at around 1.8m (6ft) or so, and has broad pinnate leaves of greyish green. These can add an air of the exotic to the most mundane setting and this plant offers the added advantage of being hardy down to minus double figures. Although *Phormium tenax* is a commonly used garden plant, it has many colourful and compact cultivars that make excellent container subjects, such as 'Bronze Baby', whilst the cascading, yellow banded *Phormium cookianum* 'Cream Delight' is another excellent container subject. For a dry sunny spot, *Agave americana* is perfect, although children and pets may need protection from its fearsome spines – a well placed bottle cork normally does the trick!

Succulents

For the ultimate in low maintenance containers, plant shallow clay 'pans' with succulents such as house leeks (Sempervivum) and Lewisia, which require little irrigation and no feeding. To create an impact these are best displayed in quantity: use old railway sleepers or chunky pieces of timber to create staging so that the pans can be placed three or four deep. House leeks produce offsets readily, so it is possible to bulk up numbers and increase your display with minimal outlay (see Propagating From Plantlets, page 95). Succulents are also a good choice for growing in windowboxes.

Vegetables

Further details of using vegetables in containers can be found in the chapter Growing Plants for Food, but essentially most of the fast growing annual crops such as salad leaves, chilli and capsicum peppers, and dwarf and trailing tomato are suitable for growing in containers or windowboxes.

Spring bulbs

There is more information on planting bulbs in containers in the chapter Planting Techniques (pages 62–75), and spring bulbs make excellent container subjects if planted with an evergreen centre piece such as a fastigiated (upright with tight foliage) conifer, compact Skimmia or even an ornamental grass. Dwarf daffodils (Narcissus), crocuses, snowdrops (Galanthus) and *Sternbergia lutea* are all suitable for containers and windowboxes, brightening patios and walls with their vibrant spring colours.

Autumn bulbs

Exotic autumn bulbs such as *Nerine bowdenii*, *Tulbaghia violacea* and *Amaryllis* 'Johannesburg' can be difficult to grow in gardens that are cool and damp, but planted in a container or windowbox with gritty compost and set out in a hot sunny spot, they should do well, especially when combined with other sun loving plants of a compact nature such as *Artemisia* 'Powis Castle' or *Ceratostigma griffithii*.

Grouping different types of plants in a variety of pots is an effective way of creating instant colour in the garden

Winter interest

A container planted with a stem colour shrub such as *Cornus* 'Midwinter Fire' or *Rubus thibetanus* 'Silver Fern' with the ornamental grass *Pennisetum alopecuroides* 'Hameln', or *Chasmanthium latifolium* and trailing variegated ivy will provide plenty of interest during the winter months. As all of these plants can then be planted into permanent positions in the garden, it is a good way of using recently purchased plants over winter before planting out. Other good plants for winter containers are *Cyclamen persicum* and *Solanum pseudocapsicum*.

Spring bulbs look wonderful planted on their own or around a central evergreen foliage plant

Hanging Baskets

Hanging baskets offer another opportunity for planting and are especially useful for covering up an unattractive wall or building. They come in a variety of sizes and styles, and which you choose will very much depend upon whether you need it to be easily lifted down for watering, and how strong the support is – a bracket fixed to a brick wall will be able to take more weight than, say, a hook screwed into the eaves.

Traditional hanging basket plants are much the same as those used in traditional containers, primarily annual bedding plants, and certainly a basket filled with trailing petunias is quite a sight. But, as with containers and window boxes you might want to consider trying less obvious plants. Succulents in particular can make a very unusual and dynamic hanging basket display to wow the neighbours.

The onset of winter need not mean that your garden is bereft of colour. Create winter mixtures in containers

Step-by-step planting

First of all, place the empty hanging basket on a large (5 or 10 ltr/10 or 20pt) pot, on a table top. The pot will enable you to turn the basket around without damaging any plants in the base of the basket. If you do not have a suitable pot, rest the basket on the table.

1 – Line the basket with a decorative material such as fake sphagnum moss, coir fibre or a purpose-made decorative liner. Cut a round piece of plastic from an old compost bag that will sit inside the decorative lining.

2 – Put a few handfuls of compost, mixed with wetting agent, into the base of the basket.

3 – Begin to plant the base of the basket with trailing plants. Push the plants through the plastic lining – having first cut a hole – and the outer decorative lining, and to help do this and protect the plants wrap the foliage of the plant in a square of plastic cut from a compost bag.

It is essential to keep hanging baskets well irrigated at all times, as plant will dry out quickly

4 – Once you have planted one 'ring' of plants, add a few more handfuls of compost and repeat the process, staggering the rows of plants for a more even and natural look. By the time the basket is two thirds full of compost it will be time to put in the plants that will fill the top of the basket. Water the basket thoroughly after hanging, to keep the weight down and make it easier to lift.

Plants for hanging baskets

Summer display
main plants: Pelargonium, *Chlorophytum comosum* (spider plant), Impatiens (busy Lizzies), Begonia

trailing plants: annuals or half-hardy plants, including Plectranthus, trailing Lobelia, Petunia and bedding Verbena

Winter display
main plants: compact conifer or young evergreen shrub as a centrepiece, along with pansies (Viola)

trailing plant: small-leaved ivy (Hedera)

1

2

3

4

Water Gardening

Water brings something truly special to a garden: movement, sound, reflection, new planting opportunities and plenty of wildlife. In fact, a body of water is the single most important feature for encouraging wildlife into your garden, with all the benefits that can bring.

Water features set off certain plantings to great effect; for example the dark red stems of *Cornus alba* 'Sibirica' and golden yellow branches of *Salix alba* var. *vitellina* 'Britzensis' can look absolutely lovely when reflected in the still water of a pool on a sunny winter day. Similarly the often fiery flowers of Astilbe, cheery yellow flowers of marsh marigold *Caltha palustris* or variegated leaves of water iris sit perfectly in the watery scene, as these marginal or moisture loving plants were made for this environment.

However, water can also be tricky to manage and the problems of blanket weed, duck weed and algal bloom are likely to be all too familiar to gardeners with water features. However, a good balance of plants and knowledge of basic water management can help to reduce the incidences of such nuisance plants.

Types of Water Feature

Depending on the size of your garden and what you want to use it for, water features can be almost any size. Even the smallest garden can have water in it, indeed some gardeners convert almost all of their available space into a water feature, installing stepping stones or bridges to allow access around the garden.

Formal pond

Ponds can be formal or informal, and the style of your garden and personal taste will dictate which you choose. A formal pond is usually straight sided or geometric in design, the sides often constructed of hard landscape materials such as stone or brick, which are sometimes raised. Decorative fountains and cascades are very much part of the formal pond, as are formal cascades. The planting in a formal pond will often be quite restrained and controlled – a water lily, floating plants and oxygenators – but the hard landscaped edges often mean that marginal plants and bog plants cannot feature.

> **TIP**
>
> You can also purchase ready-made self-contained water features, usually half barrels or containers with a built-in pump and decorative 'spout' from which water flows. Even a bird bath can act as a garden water feature.

Informal pond

An informal pond is, unsurprisingly, far more relaxed in design, with few or no straight edges which tend to be natural in composition: either grass running straight to the water's edge, or informal hard landscape materials such as rocks or rustic timbers. Cascades or waterfalls need to be executed carefully in an informal setting if they are not to look contrived, and fountains tend to look rather incongruous in an informal pond.

A water feature can be as elaborate or as simple as your personal taste dictates

Self-contained water features

In addition to ponds there are also other water features that can help to bring a garden to life. For example, self-contained water features can easily be constructed in most garden settings.

You will need a large plastic bin let into the ground to act as the reservoir. Set a

There are many different self-contained water features now available on the market

submersible pump into this reservoir and fill it with water. Then cover over the top of the reservoir with reinforcing mesh (of the type used in reinforced concrete) and then a finer mesh, with the outlet pipe from the reservoir coming through the mesh. The mesh can then be covered with different sized cobbles and stones, and the outlet pipe either held in place by these stones or passed through a specially drilled rock (widely available at garden centres). When the pump is turned on, the water from the reservoir is drawn up through the feature rock to trickle back into the reservoir. You will need regularly to top up the water in the reservoir.

Constructing a Pond

Ponds are typically constructed using one of three different techniques: by using a butyl rubber or synthetic liner; by laying a concrete/screed base, a job best left to the professionals; or by fitting a pre-formed GRP (glass reinforced plastic) liner.

Preparing the site

Whatever technique you decide to employ, the initial preparation is the same. Mark out the shape of the pond on the ground. For informal ponds you could use a hose pipe or length of rope laid onto the ground and manoeuvred into position until you are happy with the shape. With a GRP liner, lay the liner upside down on the ground and mark around the shape using spray paint or sand. When marking out the shape of your pond, remember to allow for a level edge of around 40cm (16in) width all the way around the pond. Decide where your shallow and deep ends will be.

Remove any turf to compost, and begin excavating the pond, remembering to create a shallow end and a deep end. If you are using a butyl liner, you should think about making shelves inside the pond onto which aquatic plants can be placed. These can be simply constructed by cutting away the soil to form a step inside the pond. GRP liners come with these shelves already built in to them.

Once you have reached the required depth, go over the site again to remove any stones that might puncture the liner or damage the GRP. At this point the next phase will depend on the type of liner you are using.

Butyl rubber or synthetic liner

Line the excavated pond with either sharp sand, old carpet, newspapers or purpose-made pond under-liner. This will protect the liner from being punctured by sharp stones.

Take great care to ensure that you do not puncture your butyl liner in the process of making your pond

To work out how big the liner should be, use this calculation:

(depth at the deepest point) 2 + length
X (depth at the deepest point) 2 + width

For example, a pond with a depth of 1m (3ft), a width of 3m (10ft) and a length of 5m (16ft) will need a liner that is 35m (115ft) square, and although at this size there will inevitably be some off-cuts, it is far better to have a liner that is too big rather than one that is a shade too small!

Place the butyl liner into the pond, smoothing out the worst of the creases, and begin filling it with water, which will further reduce creasing in the liner.

Pre-formed liners are available in many shapes and sizes. However, digging the hole to accommodate one of these is not always that easy

Pond essentials

Location Ponds are generally best located in full sun and away from trees that will drop leaves into the water. In this way water quality will be maintained at the best possible level.

On the level Try to build on a level site if possible. Building on an uneven site presents difficulties as water, of course, will always find its level, and the resultant exposed sides can look odd.

Water circulation is important to keep the water healthy and oxygen levels high. In a large body of water this need is reduced as the sheer volume helps to maintain a balance, but in small ponds a pump running a cascade or fountain will help greatly.

Pump capacity If you are using a pond pump, make sure the capacity of the pump is suitable for the amount of water in your pond. A GRP (glass-reinforced plastic) liner will be 'rated' to show its capacity, and if you are using a butyl liner the pump supplier will be able to calculate the capacity based on the size of the liner. The pump supplier will also want to know the 'head of lift', that is the depth at which the pump will sit and the height to which water will need to be pumped.

Spawning grounds Build your pond with a shallow end and a deep end to create different planting and wildlife zones. At least part of the pond should be 1m (3ft) deep to maintain water quality. If possible have at least one part of the pond where the base rises up to close to ground level, to enable amphibians (and any unlucky mammals that might accidentally fall in) to escape.

Pre-formed GRP liner

Line the excavated pond with either sharp sand, old carpet, newspapers or purpose-made pond under-liner. Place the GRP liner in the lined, excavated pit, half fill with water to settle the liner and back fill around the sides with soil dug from the pond, firming the soil in regularly.

Filling your pond

The best way to fill a pond is with natural rainwater, which, unlike tap water, is not treated with chemicals and is therefore more suitable for wildlife, fish and plants. Ponds can also be 'seeded' by taking a bucketful of water from an existing pond – however, always ask permission before doing this – and adding it to your pond. The micro-organisms in the water from the existing pond will help to populate your new pond quickly with beneficial bacteria and bugs of all descriptions.

Making the pond edge

How you construct the edge of your pond will have a real impact on how successfully it 'sits' in the garden. This is especially important with informal ponds if they are not to look contrived, whilst a formal pond is easier, as it is, by definition, an artificial edifice. A formal pond can be edged with stone flags, concrete slabs, raised bricks and so on. An informal pond can be edged with rock or informally laid slabs, but the method I favour is using either plants, turf or cobbles to blend the edge seamlessly into the garden.

Turf can be laid over the edge of the pond and just into the water to create a smooth transition from lawn to pond.

Wildflowers or cultivated plants can be sown or planted 'over' the edge to make the transition from dry land to marginal plants.

Cobbles can be laid onto the shallow edges, and these can be inter-planted with marginal plants.

Keeping the Water Clear

Anyone who already has a pond will appreciate the importance of keeping the water clear, and the difficulties experienced in achieving it sometimes. Water quality is affected by a number of factors:

Pond location As already mentioned, in general a pond in full sun, not under trees, is better than a shady pond.

Organic matter A build up of leaves and detritus can lead to poisonous gases being expelled, which can have a negative effect on water quality and kill fish and wildlife. Dredging the bottom of the pond will help to remove rotting material.

Weather conditions In very hot weather it is common for ponds to form an algal 'bloom', which can appear as a green or white film on the water surface. This is sometimes associated with poor oxygen levels in the water. This can be reduced by spraying water over the pond in the cool of the evening, which will help to increase oxygen levels.

Balanced planting Getting the right balance of plants will help to keep the water clear. Obtaining a balanced planting in your

A pond vacuum cleaner is a useful device for removing debris from the surface of the water

Oxygenating plants like Elodea are necessary to help keep water clear

TIP There are a number of treatments available that can be applied to the water surface to help keep the water clear. Some of these are organic, bacterial solutions or crystals and others are chemical. Ask your supplier for advice.

pond will help with water quality and clarity, and create a more natural environment for fish and wildlife. A healthy pond will have around one third of its surface area covered by aquatic plants with floating leaves such as water lilies, and will also contain oxygenating plants, floating plants and marginal plants.

Fish Too many fish in a pond have a negative impact on water quality, as they will often eat almost every living thing in the pond – apart from themselves.

Invasive weeds These include blanket weed and duck weed, which are often associated with new ponds and should be systematically removed by skimming with a net or, in the case of blanket weed by winding out with a forked stick.

Wild fauna A good balance of wildlife helps to keep water healthy, with some animals, water snails for example, actively taking the role of cleaners.

New ponds will always go through a settling in period, when water quality can fluctuate and weeds will proliferate. Be patient!

Pond Life

One of the main reasons for having a garden pond is to introduce a new range of flora and fauna to the garden scene. For children, wildlife ponds provide the most wonderful learning opportunities, as pond dipping (in the company of an adult, and making sure no animals are harmed) is almost like a mini safari in your own back garden.

Ornamental fish

Ornamental fish have always been tremendously popular with gardeners, and golden Orf, Koi carp and goldfish are common additions to ponds. But for the health of the pond and the fish themselves, it is essential to get the right balance; too many fish will de-naturize the pond and compromise their own health.

There are no hard and fast rules on the right numbers of fish for a pond, as so much depends on the style of the pond, the planting and the depth of the water. Fish growth is very much affected by the amount of space they have available to them, as well as available food.

Whatever you do, bear in mind that fish need looking after. For example, fish that are affected by illness may need to be put to

A plastic mesh will stop leaves and debris from falling into your pond

Wildlife do's and don'ts

If you want your pond to be primarily a wildlife pond, follow these tips:

- **Don't** have too many fish, or if possible have no fish at all. Fish eat the larval or egg stages of many pond animals and can dramatically affect the wildlife level.
- **Do** have a 'beach' area of cobbles or rocks where amphibians can spawn and creatures can easily get in and out of the water.
- **Don't** allow leaves to build up in the pond too much, skim them off the surface as they fall. If they do settle to the bottom then leave them be; stirring them up will release harmful gases like methane.

Fish can be detrimental in a wildlife pond, as they are the major predators for emerging larvae

sleep, and it is worth taking these considerations on board before buying and stocking your pond with fish.

Other fauna

One thing that will happen to your pond, whether you want it to or not, is its rapid population by wildlife, from tiny micro-organisms to 'mini-beasts' such as dragonfly larvae and magnificent diving beetles. Many insects rely on water for the egg and larval stages of their young. Amphibians such as frogs, toads and newts need water to spawn in. All of these animals help to either improve water quality, control garden pests or create a balance in the garden through predation.

Pests, Diseases & Problems

By creating a beautiful garden full of lovely plants we are also creating a feast of tasty food for pests, and a spawning ground for diseases. There are also cultural problems that can arise from prevalent conditions, for example strong winds. All of which can seem rather daunting, particularly for the beginner.

However, all of the information we have gathered so far should illustrate one thing very clearly: that well chosen, well grown, healthy plants will always be far less susceptible to pests and diseases than ill chosen and poorly grown specimens. So all of the skill and knowledge that you put into your garden, and the learning you employ to help you get there, helps to create the healthiest possible environment.

A well balanced garden is far more likely to be healthy than one where chemical controls are used as a matter of course to control pests and diseases, so try to limit the use of chemicals and allow nature the opportunity to address the problem first. Use the table and descriptions in this section to correctly identify the problem before taking any necessary action – if any is needed.

Troubleshooting

These diagrams are designed to help you diagnose the conditions you may find in your garden from the symptoms you can see. Starting with the part of the plant that appears to be most affected, by answering successive questions 'yes' [✓] or 'no' [✗] you will quickly arrive at a probable cause. Once you have identified the cause, turn to the relevant entry in the directory of pests and diseases for how to treat the problem.

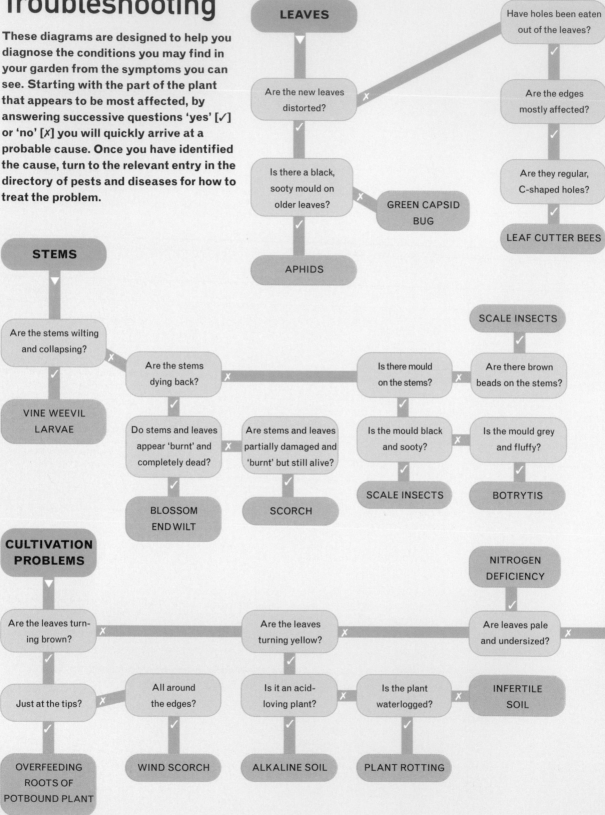

LEAVES

Have holes been eaten out of the leaves?

Are the new leaves distorted?

Are the edges mostly affected?

Is there a black, sooty mould on older leaves?

GREEN CAPSID BUG

Are they regular, C-shaped holes?

LEAF CUTTER BEES

APHIDS

STEMS

SCALE INSECTS

Are the stems wilting and collapsing?

Are the stems dying back?

Is there mould on the stems?

Are there brown beads on the stems?

VINE WEEVIL LARVAE

Do stems and leaves appear 'burnt' and completely dead?

Are stems and leaves partially damaged and 'burnt' but still alive?

Is the mould black and sooty?

Is the mould grey and fluffy?

BLOSSOM END WILT

SCORCH

SCALE INSECTS

BOTRYTIS

CULTIVATION PROBLEMS

NITROGEN DEFICIENCY

Are the leaves turning brown?

Are the leaves turning yellow?

Are leaves pale and undersized?

Just at the tips?

All around the edges?

Is it an acid-loving plant?

Is the plant waterlogged?

INFERTILE SOIL

OVERFEEDING ROOTS OF POTBOUND PLANT

WIND SCORCH

ALKALINE SOIL

PLANT ROTTING

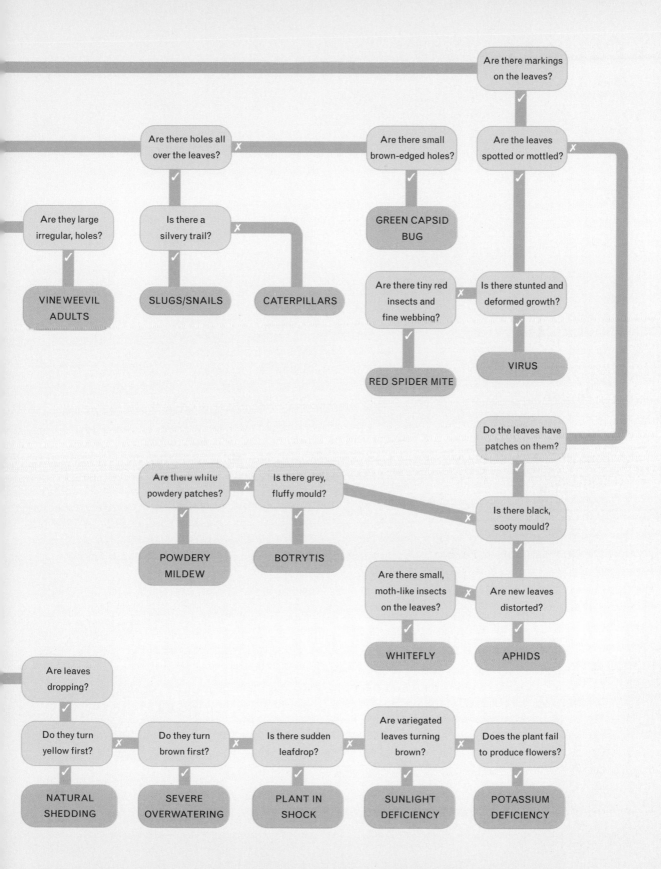

Are there markings on the leaves? ✓

Are there holes all over the leaves? ✗

Are there small brown-edged holes? ✓ → GREEN CAPSID BUG

Are the leaves spotted or mottled? ✓ / ✗

Are they large irregular, holes? ✓ → VINE WEEVIL ADULTS

Is there a silvery trail? ✓ → SLUGS/SNAILS ✗ → CATERPILLARS

Are there tiny red insects and fine webbing? ✓ → RED SPIDER MITE

Is there stunted and deformed growth? ✓ → VIRUS

Do the leaves have patches on them? ✓

Are there white powdery patches? ✗ Is there grey, fluffy mould?

Is there black, sooty mould? ✗ / ✓

✓ POWDERY MILDEW ✓ BOTRYTIS

Are there small, moth-like insects on the leaves? ✗ Are new leaves distorted?

✓ WHITEFLY ✓ APHIDS

Are leaves dropping? ✓

Do they turn yellow first? ✗ Do they turn brown first? ✗ Is there sudden leafdrop? ✗ Are variegated leaves turning brown? ✗ Does the plant fail to produce flowers?

✓ NATURAL SHEDDING
✓ SEVERE OVERWATERING
✓ PLANT IN SHOCK
✓ SUNLIGHT DEFICIENCY
✓ POTASSIUM DEFICIENCY

Pests, Diseases & Problems

Inevitably, any garden will suffer occasional problems that affect the quality and growth of plants and crops. Part of this is due to the very nature of garden plants, many of which are non-native and therefore bring with them their own range of problems that are sometimes exacerbated in a garden setting.

Pests can range from specific insect pests that affect only one group of plants, such as lily beetle, to non-specific pests that might trouble a range of plants – squirrels, for example. The main disease problems for plants are either fungal or viral. Fungal diseases are often associated with weather conditions, either damp and warm or on occasion excessively hot, and can be passed from plant to plant by pollinating insects. Viral conditions are also often passed around by insects. Excessive heat, wind, water-logging are all cultural problems that can damage and kill plants. Poor nutrient levels and inadequate soil cultivation can also have an adverse effect on plant growth and health. Weeds exacerbate cultural problems as they compete with garden plants for nutrients, water, light and space.

Pests

Many of the problems that affect plants can be offset right at the start, by the way plants are grouped together, and how they are planted and maintained. For example, a garden that has one predominant plant – roses, perhaps – will always be prone to specific diseases, whereas a garden with a mixture of plants tends to be more balanced and less likely to suffer problems. I had first-hand experience of this in a garden that had a large collection of ornamental crab apples, over 500 plants in all. A few trees became infected with blossom end wilt that is spread by pollinating insects and makes the leaves and stems shrivel and die. With so many trees planted closely together, the disease went from one to another in no time, devastating the collection. So, remember to follow these simple points and your garden will be less likely to suffer from problems:

• Choose the right plants for your conditions.
• Plant them properly, having cultivated the soil well.
• Look after them in times of extreme weather, as a stressed plant is more likely to suffer from pests or diseases than a healthy one.
• Try to avoid monocultures – plantings dominated by one type of plant – as mixed plantings tend to be far healthier.
• Keep an eye out for problems, not just pests and diseases but also areas where drainage is slow after heavy rain, for example. Observation of natural conditions will help you to anticipate problems before they become impossible to fix.
• Timely intervention is really important, as the earlier that a problem can be tackled the greater the chances of success.

Slugs and snails

Slugs and snails are nocturnal feeders, especially obvious after rainfall or heavy dew. They leave tell-tale silvery slime trails wherever they go. The damage they cause can be extensive on some, favoured plants, and usually affects the leaves and stems of plants in the form of holes, tears or complete shredding of leaves.

Slugs and snails are predated by frogs, toads, hedgehogs, song thrush and other birds, so don't poison them with slug pellets as you will pass this poison on into the food chain. Instead, use sharp mulches around plants that are prone to attack – sharp gravel, crushed shells – put plants such as Hosta in containers with petroleum jelly around the rim (slugs and snails won't cross this), pick the offenders off by hand and release them into the wild, and make your garden as friendly as possible for the predators.

Aphids

Aphids feed on soft plant growth, sucking the sap – causing a distinctive puckering on the leaves – and leaving behind a sticky substance called honeydew, which then becomes affected by a black, dusty mould known as sooty mould. Aphids are also virus vectors, transmitting viruses from one plant to another through the sap they ingest. Aphids are a major food source for ladybirds, lacewings, hoverfly larvae and many birds, all of which will help to control aphid numbers if given a little time to do so. Localized infestations can be treated by either removing and squashing by hand, spraying with soapy water (this blocks the aphids' breathing apparatus) or with a careful, targeted application of herbicide. Organic barrier sprays such as liquid garlic, which make plants taste unpalatable, may also help.

Red spider mites

Red spider mites are tiny, sap sucking insects that can cause a large amount of damage, and even plant death. Although they are very small they spin a silky web to help protect them and enable them to move around the host plant. If the infestation is especially bad these webs are highly visible. Red spider mites are primarily a problem for house and greenhouse plants, although they can attack plants on hot, dry and sheltered walls and fences. There is a biological control for red spider mite called *Phytoseilus persimilis* which is highly effective at controlling this pest. You could also try organic barrier sprays.

Mealy bugs

Mealy bugs are white, 'furry' insects that hang onto plants and suck the sap from the stems; they tend to look rather like miniature furry barnacles.

Ladybird larvae and adults will feed on them, particularly in the warme months, but there are no other effective controls as the 'fur' protects them from most chemicals.

Whitefly

Whitefly are mainly glasshouse pests, affecting crop plants such as tomatoes but also ornamental plants. Like aphids they suck sap and leave behind fungus-prone honeydew, and also like aphids they multiply at an alarming rate. The biological control *Encarsia formosa* is effective at controlling whitefly in greenhouses, especially if introduced at the first sign of infestation. Also try organic barrier sprays and organic pesticide.

Scale insects

Scale insects are sap-sucking insects that fix themselves like limpets to the stems and leaves of plants, and are protected by a scale that makes them hard to deal with. Ideally they should be scraped off when spotted, but if the infestation is severe it may be better to prune out affected branches or dispose of the plant completely.

Shield bugs

Shield bugs are large insects with iridescent green colouring and flattened, shield-shaped bodies. Although some are sap suckers the damage they cause is minimal and can largely be discounted.

Vine weevil

Vine weevil adults cause damage to leaves by eating characteristic C-shaped notches in foliage. However, it is the larvae that are more harmful, the off-white, C-shaped maggots causing damage to roots that can sometimes lead to the complete collapse and death of the plant. Adult vine weevil are largely nocturnal and can be picked off plants and squashed – although they have a habit of 'playing dead' when disturbed and will drop off the leaves and stems of plants.

There are a number of treatments for the larval stage, including parasitic nematodes that are applied as a soil or compost drench.

Capsid bugs

Capsid bugs cause damage around the growing points (buds) and leaf axils of plants. The damage is characterised by reddish brown spots that gradually enlarge to become holes in the leaves. Capsid bugs are sap suckers but also have toxic saliva which adds to the damage on the host plant. They can be removed by hand or treated with organic pesticide, also try organic barrier sprays.

Scale insects

Scale insects are sap-sucking insects that fix themselves like limpets to the stems and leaves of plants, and are protected by a scale that makes them hard to deal with. Ideally they should be scraped off when spotted, but if the infestation is severe it may be better to prune out affected branches or dispose of the plant completely.

Cutworms

Cutworms are the soil dwelling larvae of a number of insects, including moths such as the turnip moth. They usually have soft, maggot-like bodies and noticeable mouth parts with which they nibble through the roots of plants and grasses.

In extreme infestations, particularly on lawns, water the lawn well and then cover for 24 hours with plastic or tarpaulin. The cutworms will be drawn to the surface and when the cover is removed can either be swept up or left as a tasty snack for the birds.

Leaf miners

Leaf miners are they larvae of a number of species of flying insect, which eat tunnels between the upper and lower 'skins' of leaves.

Although the damage can be a little unsightly they are hardly plant enemy number one, and can be left alone.

Capsid bugs leave behind them their poisonous saliva, which kills young plant cells

Beneficial Insects

Beneficial insects can help in the battle against pests by creating a natural balance through predation. The key to encouraging these 'good' insects into your garden – and biodiversity in all its forms – lies in providing a range of habitats and food sources. The way you choose to maintain your garden can have a massive impact on insect life. Plants that are rich in pollen and nectar, such as hardy Salvia, Verbena bonariensis, Sedum, Eupatorium, Phlomis and Nepeta will attract insects that rely on these food sources, and in many instances the larvae of these insects will repay your kindness by eating pests. Shrubs and trees that produce fruit and berries, including crab apple (Malus sylvestris), deciduous Viburnum and cherry (Prunus) will also provide food for bugs, as well as birds and mammals.

Making some modest changes to the maintenance of your garden can have great benefits for bugs. The traditional autumn 'cut down and clear up' deprives many insects of winter hideouts – not to mention removing seed heads that provide food for other animals. Leaving plants standing through winter and cutting them back in early spring provides plenty of suitable habitats for wildlife, and has aesthetic benefits too.

Ladybirds
Ladybirds are distinctive insects and a great gardener's friend, as most species eat aphids in both adult and larval stages. Although the adults are easily recognisable, the larvae are not and can often be mistaken for pests and killed, which is a terrible shame given that they can eat up to 400 aphids before they pupate. Ladybird boxes are available to buy that can help the adults to overwinter.

Devil's coach horse
The Devil's coach horse is a distinctive black beetle that predates garden pests such as cutworms, leatherjackets and slugs. It needs places to shelter in between its roving hunting runs, so log piles, paving slabs and upturned pots make ideal habitats.

Bumble bees
Bumblebees are important pollinators of garden plants and crops. Their ability to fly earlier in the year and in poorer weather than honey bees makes them all the more useful. They nest in holes in the ground but can be helped with an upturned clay pot filled with moss, which makes an excellent nest.

Hover flies
Hoverflies come in many shapes and sizes, but in most cases both the adult and larval stages of hoverflies eat aphids making them a real friend to any gardener.

Green lace-wing
This small lacy-winged insect has transparent wings with green veins and it is this that gives it its name. The larvae of lacewings eat large numbers of aphids. The adults feed on nectar and it lays eggs in quiet, undisturbed nooks and crannies.

Brown centi-pede
Brown centipede needs the same kind of sheltering spots as the Devil's Coach Horse when it isn't living and hunting just below the surface of the soil, preying on soil insects with its fearsome jaws.

Tachinid flies
There are many species of tachinid flies, and most of them parasitize caterpillars with their eggs, with hatch into larvae and then eat their host from the inside out before pupating. Adults feed on the honeydew of aphids and scale insects

Diseases

Viral diseases are most often transmitted from infected plants to healthy plants via sap-sucking insects (referred to as virus vectors). Once a plant is infected there are no cures, but by guarding against insect pests and taking swift action when they attack you should be able to minimise the risk. Fungal diseases are usually most prevalent in conditions were air circulation is poor and the atmosphere damp and warm. Wherever possible try to avoid growing conditions that will encourage fungal diseases by:
• Keeping greenhouses well ventilated.
• Pruning shrubs to create an open shape that will aid air circulation.
• Avoiding over-planting that can create areas where air circulation is poor.
• Improving drainage and using mound planting techniques
Good hygiene will help to prevent the spread of fungal diseases, including:
• Tidying up fallen, affected leaves and removing badly affected leaves.
• Regular soil cultivation to keep the surface dry and less suitable for spores to proliferate in.
• Pruning out badly affected woody material.
• Disposing of infested plants.
All infected material should be burned, never put it on the compost heap.

Powdery mildew

Powdery mildew forms as a powdery white patch on the top side of the leaves of affected plants, eventually covering the whole leaf and often the stems too. As with all moulds and fungal diseases its appearance is often associated with climatic conditions as moulds and fungal diseases tend to thrive in either warm and damp or sometimes hot and dry conditions. Treat with a fungicide and remove fallen and badly infected leaves, and destroy severely afflicted plants.

Phytophtora

Phytophtora fungi are water borne soil-based fungi of numerous species that affect a wide range of plants. Phytophtora root disease affect the roots of many plants and usually results in death, but is notoriously difficult to isolate and, as it has similar symptoms to cultural conditions such as water-logging, it is often hard to be certain that it is the cause of the problem. Poor drainage certainly aids the spread of phytophtora root disease, as does flooding. Infected plants either defoliate or, in the case of evergreens, turn yellow and/or brown. There is no treatment available.

Rust

Rust is a fungal disease that leaves characteristic orange, brown or yellow spores on the leaves and stems of infected plants and can lead to defoliation. Treat with a fungicide and remove fallen and badly infected leaves, prune out affected wood and destroy severely afflicted plants.

Coral spot

Coral spot is closely associated with damaged, dead or dying wood, which become covered with pinkish pustules. It rarely causes serious damage to plants but should be pruned out when spotted and the prunings burned.

Botrytis

Botrytis is usually referred to as grey mould, and can affect greenhouse crops such as tomatoes and also outdoor plants that produce lots of soft, sappy growth. It can affect all of the top growth of a plant, resulting in rotting. Cut back to healthy material.

Sooty mould

Sooty mould forms on the honeydew excreted by sap-sucking insects. Controlling the insect themselves will prevent sooty mould from forming, otherwise remove affected leaves and clear up fallen leaves.

Blossom end wilt

Blossom end wilt particularly affects flowering trees and shrubs from the family Rosaceae, including flowering cherries (Prunus) and crab and culinary apples (Malus). Spread by pollinating insects the symptoms appear after flowering, when leaves and shoots die back and look as if they have be burned with a blow torch. Prune back affected branches into uninfected tissue.

Viral diseases

Viral diseases Symptoms include streaked or mottled leaves and stunted or deformed growth. Unfortunately, they are impossible to cure but effective pest control will help to protect plants as viruses are most often transmitted by sap-sucking insects, such as aphids and whitefly.

Cultural Problems

Poor growing conditions often cause unhealthy looking plants, and these plants will be more susceptible to attack from pests and diseases. By ensuring each plant receives the correct amount of light, water and nutrients – and is adequately protected from factors such as wind and cold – you will give your garden a head start against other problems. Often, the best way to grow healthy plants is to avoid planting the wrong plants in the wrong place.

Water logging

Waterlogging can cause damage to plants and often result in death. The fine feeder roots of plants are highly prone to damage by waterlogging and can often rot away completely. The resultant symptoms include wilting of foliage and partial or total defoliation, followed by plant death.

Nutrient deficiency

Nutrient deficiencies can disclour foliage and stunt growth. In all cases soil improvement and adding organic matter will improve conditions. Nitrogen and phosphorus deficiencies have similar symptoms such as pale or yellow foliage turning red and falling prematurely. Potassium deficiency is typified by yellowing to the leaf margins which then turns brown

Scorch

Scorch can be caused by drying winds, excessive sun (particularly in plants with thin or light leaves) or sea spray. Leaves can wilt or burn around the edges and may drop. Herbicide spray drift in rural areas can cause similar symptoms. Put vulnerable plants in sheltered spots, use salt spray tolerant plants.

Frost damage

Damage is caused by the freezing and thawing of – particularly – soft, sappy spring growth. The more rapid the thawing, the worse the damage, which usually results in the dying back of leaves, shoots and flowers. Protect plants with fleece or grow in sheltered locations.

Drought

The rapid wilting of leaves and stems is sometimes accompanied by scorch. Plants may wilt during the heat of the day and recover at night when temperatures drop. Choose drought-tolerant plants for dry, hot gardens, and use mulches, good preparation and wetting agents when planting vulnerable plants.

Types of Weed Treatment

One definition of a weed is 'a wild plant or herb in the wrong place', and this is probably as good a definition as any, although the wild part could be augmented with ornamentals too, as many have the potential to be so successful as to become problematic.

Weeds are generally considered to be unwanted native plants that are aggressive and persistent, as opposed to our perception of native wildflowers, which may technically be no different to 'weeds', but are a long way away from weeds.

So, let us consider weeds to be unwanted, aggressive and persistent native or introduced plants, to separate them from desirable wildflowers. Weeds are either perennial or annual, the majority herbaceous but a few woody.

Their aggressive and persistent nature is what makes them problematic for gardeners, as they compete for soil nutrients and water, fight ornamentals for light, and physically overwhelm them. Weeds can also make soil difficult to cultivate and, of course, look unsightly.

Perennial weeds

Perennial weeds are just like perennial ornamental plants in that their life cycle is longer than one season. Herbaceous perennial weeds regenerate from the root stock each season. Perennial weeds can be tough to control as they often have extensive root systems to support their top growth and can grow back rapidly if the top growth if removed by, for example, hoeing. Common perennial weeds include: bindweed; bramble; couch grass (right); creeping buttercup; ground elder; horsetail; and stinging nettle.

Annual weeds

Annual weeds have a life cycle of less than one season, and in the case of some a life cycle of mere weeks. This is the secret to their success, as they can rapidly colonize large areas of ground by germinating, flowering and setting seed over and over again in just one season. Although they are comparatively easy to remove – by hoeing or hand weeding, for example – their seed can persist in soil for years, ready to invade again. Common annual weeds include: annual meadow grass; cleavers; groundsel (right); hairy bittercress; redshank; and shepherd's purse.

Chemical treatment

Not too long ago there was a wide range of herbicides available for amateur use, but this is no longer the case as new legislation is introduced banning the use of certain chemicals that are deemed to be unsafe to the environment.

It is likely that this process will continue over the coming years and that amateur – and indeed professional – gardeners will need to look toward more sustainable methods of weed control rather than chemical use.

There are, however, some herbicides still available to use and when applied in a sensible and sensitive way they do undoubtedly add to the gardener's armoury. The chemical most often used and most widely available is glyphosate which is sold under a variety of trade names. Glyphosate is a systemic herbicide (see below) and is considered very safe to use as, providing it is applied correctly, it is taken up rapidly by the plant.

Contact herbicides

Contact herbicides kill off the parts of weeds that are touched by the chemical. They are fast acting and, because of this, are most suitable for the control of annual weeds, especially on unplanted ground or on paths and drives.

Systemic herbicides

Systemic herbicides are absorbed by the plant and transferred around it by the plants own vascular system. They are slower to act than contact herbicides and tend to need slightly warmer conditions as the treated plant must be actively growing in order for the chemical to work. Systemic herbicides are ideally suited to the control of perennial weeds.

Persistent herbicides

Persistent herbicides stay on the surface of the ground and prevent the germination of weeds. There are very few of these chemicals still available as they are the least environmentally friendly, getting into water courses and ultimately into drinking water.

There are many ways to get rid of weeds like this creeping buttercup, but try to use a method which is environmentally friendly

Cultural Controls

Chief among the cultural control methods is weeding – either hand weeding where the plant is removed roots and all by hand pulling, or weeding using a hoe, which cuts the tops from the weeds but leaves the roots intact. Hand weeding has the advantage that all of the weed is removed, but is time consuming and not really suitable for large areas.

It can also be tough to hand weed perennial weeds with really deep and extensive root systems, and these will usually need to be dug out.

Hoeing is much quicker and involves removing the top growth of the weed by severing it from the roots. Carried out in hot weather, this control method is very effective at restricting annual weeds, as the severed tops will wilt rapidly in the sun and the roots die off in the ground. However, it is hard to control perennial weeds using hoeing alone, as they soon regenerate from the root stock, although regular hoeing will certainly help to reduce the strength and vigour of perennial weeds.

There are other several other cultural methods that can be employed to control weeds, which are listed below.

Physical barriers — Physical barriers such as old carpet or tarpaulin can be placed on top of areas infested with pernicious perennial weeds. In doing so the light is excluded from the leaves, preventing photosynthesis and causing the top growth to die back. However, some weeds are so persistent that even after 12 months of this treatment they can still regenerate from the roots system, and may need to be cut back and re-covered for a further period of time.

Mulches — Mulches, planting fabric and mulch mats can help to suppress weed growth, but they are always most effective when the soil has been as thoroughly cleared and weeded as possible before the application of mulching materials.

Cut X-shaped holes in mulching membranes to allow plants access whilst keeping weeds in check

Brushcutters — Brushcutting is a quick and effective way of removing the tops of woody weeds, which can then be dug out or covered up with a physical barrier.

Petrol-engined brushcutters are effective but expensive. Most plant hire shops will be able to supply suitable equipment. Protective clothing, including appropriate headgear, should always be worn.

Flamethrowers — Flamethrowers and burners can be bought or hired to help with weed control. They are used to burn off the top growth of the plants and are useful for controlling weeds in paths and drives. However, they should not be used in planted borders, or for clearing large areas where there is a fire risk. Needless to say, there is a greater risk of personal injury and/or damage to property with flamethrowers than just about any other control method, including herbicides.

Flamethrowers are useful devices for dispensing with weedy top growth, but they are inherently dangerous to use

Glossary

Acid – a pH value of below 7.0.

Aeration – improving soil air circulation by mechanically loosening the soil.

Aerial root – a root that forms above ground on a stem.

Alkaline – a pH value above 7.0

Alpine – a high altitude plant, suitable for rock gardens.

Annual – a plant completing its life cycle within one growing season.

Aquatic plant – a plant that grows in or floats on water.

Basal – at the base of a structure or organ, e.g. leaf or stem.

Berry – the fruit surrounding a seed or seeds.

Biennial – a plant that completes its lifecycle in two years by growing in the first year and flowering in the second.

Biological control – a naturally occurring or introduced control for pests, normally in the form of nematodes or insect predators.

Bloom – flower or blossom, or a white, powdery coating found on some plants.

Bog garden – a waterlogged area suitable for plants that thrive in permanently moist soil.

Bottom heat – a method employed in propagation, heating provided at the root zone to encourage rooting.

Bract – modified leaf at the base of a flower designed to look like a large flower or petal.

Bud – the organ enclosing the immature stage of a leaf, flower, shoot.

Bulb – a modified bud growing below ground.

Bulblet – small bulb formed at the side of the parent.

Catkin – a form of inflorescence consisting of bracts and tiny flowers, usually arranged in a pendant form.

Chalky – a soil with a high level of calcium carbonate (chalk) or magnesium carbonate.

Chlorophyll – the green pigment that absorbs energy from sunlight.

Chlorosis – the loss of chlorophyll leading to leaf discolouration – yellowing – caused by mineral deficiency, disease or low light levels.

Clay – fertile, heavy soil that is moisture retentive and prone to compaction and capping.

Climber – a plant that climbs or climbs by using modified stems, leaves, roots or leaf stalks.

Coppice – to prune shrubs or trees to ground level to promote strong regeneration.

Cordon – a plant trained and restricted to one stem.

Corm – a below-ground storage organ.

Cross – interbreeding, hybridization between two or more plants.

Crown – the growing point of a plant from which new stems grow, or, the upper foliage and framework of a tree or large shrub.

Cultivar – a cultivated variety of a species.

Cutting – a section of stem, leaf or root used for propagation.

Damp down – wetting the floor of a greenhouse or conservatory to boost humidity and reduce temperatures.

Damping off – a fungal disease causing the rotting and collapse of seedlings.

Deadhead – removing old and spent flowers/flowerheads to promote further flowering or prevent seed setting.

Deciduous – plants that shed seeds annually.

Divide – propagation of plants (usually perennials) by dividing the parent crown into several sections.

Dwarf – a small or slow-growing form of plant.

Epiphyte – a plant that grows on another without acting as a parasite by taking food, water.

Ericaceous – acid loving plant/compost, plant from the family Ericaceae.

Espalier – a method of training fruit into a tree with pairs of horizontal branches from a main trunk.

Evergreen – a plant that retains its leaves over more than one season, or which retains most of its leaves over that period.

Family – primary category in plant classification, coming between order and genus.

Feathered (as in feathered maiden) – a tree with a main trunk and lateral branches furnished to the ground.

Fern – a non-flowering vascular plant, frequently with feathery fronds.

Fertilization – the sexual fusion of male and female plant elements that initiates the development of seed.

Fertilizer – organic or inorganic compounds added to the growing media to improve/alter nutrient levels.

Flower – the reproductive structure of flowering plants.

Frond – the leaf of a fern.

Fungus – non-photosynthetic, non-vascular organism including mushrooms, moulds.

Garden origin – applies to plants that have been artificially bred or selected.

Genus – primary category in plant classification, ranked between family and species.

Germination – the change that occurs when a seed develops into a young plant.

Glaucous – covered with a blue/green or blue/grey bloom.

Growing season – the part of the year in which active plant growth occurs.

Grow on – the stage after propagation when plants have been potted on and are grown for a further period before planting.

Habit – the appearance or growing tendency of a plant that gives it its characteristic form.

Harden off – to gradually acclimatize plants that have been raised in a greenhouse to the external environment.

Hardiness – the measure of reliance to frosts displayed by plants.

Hardwood – mature wood used for cutting material.

Herb – a plant with practical applications such as culinary or medicinal, or in botany any herbaceous plant.

Herbaceous – a plant that dies back to ground level at the end of the growing season and regenerates from the crown the following season.

Herbicide – chemicals used in weed control.

Humidity – the measure of air moisture content.

Humus – decomposed organic matter found in or introduced into soil/growing media.

Hybrid – a natural or artificially produced plant with two genetically distinct parents.

Infertile – soil low in nutrients or plants that do not flower due to cultural problems, disease or pests.

Inflorescence – arrangement of flowers on a single stem or axis.

Internode – a section of stem between two nodes.

Insecticide – chemical used to control insect pests.

Invasive – an aggressive plant that invades or overwhelms other plants.

Lateral – side shoot from the stem of the main plant.

Layering – a method of propagation where an attached stem is encouraged to root by laying and fixing on the soil.

Leader – the main growing stem of a plant.

Leaf – plant organ that is the primary organ in photosynthesis.

Liquid feed – a fertilizer diluted in water for application.

Loam – fertile, well drained but moisture retentive soil.

Marginal – a plant requiring permanently moist conditions, as found at the edge of a water course.

Mist – a method of increasing humidity by spraying fine droplets of water into the atmosphere or onto a plant.

Mulch – a layer of material spread on the soil surface to suppress weeds and/or improve fertility.

Native – an endemic plant that occurs naturally in an area/country.

Naturalized – introduced plants that grow as if native.

Nectar – sugary liquid secreted by some plants to attract pollinators.

Neutral – a pH of 7.0, i.e. neither acid nor alkaline.

Node – the point on a stem at which leaves, leaf buds and shoots arise.

Nut – dry fruit surrounding a single seed.

Nutrients – the minerals needed for healthy plant growth.

Offset – a small plant that forms naturally as part of a plant's vegetative growth.

Oxygenator a fully submerged aquatic plant that releases oxygen into the water.

Pan – a shallow dish used for growing alpines.

Panicle – term applied to plants with freely branched inflorescences.

Parasite – a plant that derives nutrients from another plant.

Peat – humus rich, moisture retentive decayed organic matter with a pH below 6.5.

Perennial – a plant that lives for more than two growing seasons.

Pesticide – chemicals used to control insect pests.

Petal – a modified leaf that makes up part of the flower.

pH – measure of acidity or alkalinity.

Photosynthesis – the complex series of chemical reactions in which energy from sunlight is absorbed by chlorophyll and carbon dioxide and water converted into sugars and oxygen.

Plantlet – a young, small plant that develops alongside an older one.

Pollard – to cut branches back hard to a framework or to the main trunk of a tree to restrict growth.

Pollen – grains containing the male element needed for fertilization.

Prick out – the transfer of seedlings or small cuttings into larger pots or containers.

Propagate – to increase plants by seed, cuttings, etc.

Prostrate – a plant with stems that trail or lie flat against the ground.

Respiration – absorption of oxygen and breakdown of carbohydrates, releasing carbon dioxide and water and providing energy for the plant.

Rhizome – horizontal, branching or fleshy stem growing underground or at ground level.

Rock garden – area for growing alpine plants.

Root – part of the plant that anchors it and absorbs water and nutrients from the soil or to successfully strike cuttings.

Rootball – a mass of roots and the compost or soil attached to them.

Rootstock – the underground part of a plant or the plant onto which another is grafted, as in fruit trees, roses, etc.

Rosette – the dense whorl of leaves arising from a central point or crown of a plant.

Sap – the watery fluid that runs through the conductive tissue of plants.

Scarify – removal of moss, weeds and thatch from a lawn by mechanical abrasion.

Seed head – the dried fruits of, for example, perennials.

Seedling – a young plant raised from seed.

Shoot – side growth, branch, twig or stem.

Shrub – a deciduous or evergreen woody plant with multiple stems.

Silt – moderately fertile moisture retentive soil prone to capping and compaction.

Softwood – the soft, young unripened wood of trees and shrubs.

Specimen plant – a plant grown in a prominent position, alone or with a low planting, which can be viewed from multiple angles.

Species – basic category of plant classification, ranked below genus.

Spur – short branches or branchlets along the main stem on which flowers and fruit are produced.

Standard – a tree or shrub that has been trained with a clear stem and head of foliage.

Stem – the main part of a plant, from which side stems form.

Sterile – a flower that cannot produce seeds or soil that is lacking in nutrients or has been treated to kill weed seeds.

Succulent – a plant with fleshy leaves and stems, often native to dry areas.

Tap root – a primary root, often swollen, from which the secondary root system develops.

Terminal – the end point of a stem, shoot.

Terrestrial – a plant that grows in soil.

Topiary – the clipping and training of plants into architectural or representational forms.

Train – the pruning and shaping of a tree or shrub.

Transpiration – the evaporation of water from the leaves of a plant.

Tree – a woody perennial with a crown of branches developing from a single trunk.

Variegation – the irregular pigmentation in a leaf caused by mutation or disease.

Variety – a naturally occurring variation of a species.

Vascular – containing conductive tissue that enable the passage of sap in a plant.

Waterlogged – soil that is saturated with water.

Weed – vigorous, invasive plant or any plant growing where it is not wanted.

Index

Abies koreana 27
Acer cappadocicum 'Aureum' 25
Adiantum pedatum 73
Agapanthus 'Windlebrooke' 67
Agapanthus caulescens 35
Agave americana 46, 134
Alcea rosea (Hollyhock) 12
Allium 'Globemaster' 131
Allium sphaerocephalum 131
Alpines 45
Amaryllis 'Johannesburg' 134
Anchusa 'Loddon Royalist' 67
Anchusa cespitosa 45
Annual plants 37
Anthericum lilliago 131
Aquatics 41–2
Artemisia 'Powis Castle' 86, 134
Aspect 8
Asplenium scolopendrium 73
Astilbe 137
Aubrieta 74

Barrenwort (Epimedium) 85
Bay (Laurus nobilis) 133
Beech (Fagus sylvatica) 13, 80
Begonia 136
Betula (birch) 85
Betula utilis var. jacquemontii 25
Biennial plants 38
Birch (Betula) 85
Bonsai 50
Borago officianalis 131
Border maintenance 85–8
Box (Buxus sempervirens) 13, 133
Broad leaved trees 25–6
Brush cutters 59
Bulbous plants 35–6
Buxus sempervirens (Box) 13, 133
Buying trees and shrubs 63–4
    bare root 63
    colour 64
    feathered maidens 63
    light standards 63
    pot grown and potted 64
    rootballed 64
    root systems 63
    seedlings 63
    tree size 63
    shrubs 64
    whips 63

Cacti & succulents 46
Calamagrostis x acutiflora 'Karl Foerster' 34, 133

Calendula officianalis (English marigold) 12
Caltha palustris (marsh marigold) 137
Camassia cusikii 131
Canna 'President' 35
Carpinus betulus (Hornbeam) 13, 80
Caryopteris clandonensis cultivars 86
Ceratostigma griffithii 134
Ceratostigma plumbaginoides 67
Ceratostigma willmottianum 86
Chamaerops humilis (Fishtail Palm) 134
Chasmanthium latifolium 135
Chimonanthus praecox 23
Chlorophyll 22
Clematis 'Bill MacKenzie' 83
Clematis 'Etoile Violette' 83
Clematis 'Nelly Moser' 83
Clematis 'Polish Spirit' 83
Clematis 'Silver Moon' 83
Clematis alpina 83
Clematis armandii 83
Clematis montana 83
Clematis tangutica 83
Clematis viticella hybrids 83
Climbers 39–40
Common ivy (Hedera helix) 54
Conifers 27
Container gardening 132–6
    autumn bulbs 134
    compost 133
    drainage 133
    exotica 134
    grasses 133
    hanging baskets 135–6
    hanging baskets, planting up 136
    spring bulbs 134
    succulents 134
    vegetables 134
    wetting agent 133
    what to plant 133
    winter interest 135
    winter positioning 133
Cornus 'Midwinter Fire' 135
Cornus alba 'Sibirica' 137
Cornus kousa (flowering dogwood) 23
Cornus mas 85
Corylus (harvest hazel) 85
Corylus maxima 'Purpurea' 28
Cottage garden plants 12
Crataegus laevigata 'Rosea Flora

Pleno' 25
Cultivar, variety or subspecies 24
Cyclamen persicum 135
Cymbidium 48

Dame's Violet (Hesperis matronalis) 12
Delphinium (Delphinium Belladonna group and D. Elatum group) 12
Deschampsia cespitosa 131
Deschampsia cespitosa 'Goldtau' 73
Dicksonia antartica (Tree ferns) 47, 73
Digging & general tools 57
    border fork 57
    border spade 57
    digging fork 57
    digging spade 57
    ditching/trenching spade 57
    hay fork 57
    muck or dung fork 57
    shovels 57
Digitalis purpurea Excelsior Hybrids 38
Dracaena marginata 'Tricolor' 49
Dryopteris 47
Dryopteris erythrosora 73
Dwarf daffodils (Narcissus) 134

Echinacea purpurea 131
Elaeagnus x ebbingei 'Gilt Edge' 133
Elaeagnus x ebbingei 'Maculata' 133
Elymus magellanicus 34, 133
English marigold (Calendula officianalis) 12
Epimedium (barrenwort) 85
Eschscholzia californica 37
Eupatorium purpureum 32

Fagus sylvatica (Beech) 13, 80
Fatsia japonica 28, 53
Ferns 47
Fertilizers 18
Fishtail Palm (Chamaerops humilis) 134
Flowering dogwood (Cornus kousa) 23
Flowers 22–3
Fruit 112–15
    apples 112
    dessert grapes 115

orchard fruit 112
peaches 114
pears 113
plums 113
raspberries 115
redcurrants 114
soft fruit 115

Galanthus (snowdrops) 134
Garden styles 10–15
    cottage style gardens 11–12
    formal ornamental garden 12–13
    modern ornamental garden 10–11
    naturalistic & wildlife gardens 14–15
    productive garden 13–14
Gaura lindhiemeri 30
Gentiana 'Multiflora' 45
Genus 24
Geranium 'Johnson's Blue' 67, 87
Geranium psilostemon 31
Golden Oat Grass (Stipa gigantea) 53
Greenhouse gardening 117–123
    a year in the greenhouse 122–3
    construction & siting 119
    fitting out a 120
    heating and insulation 121
    irrigation 121
    maintaining a 121
    pests and diseases, controlling 121
    staging and benching 121
    types of 118
    uses of 120
    ventilation and humidity 120
Growing fruit 108–111
Growing indoor plants 75
Growing plants for food 96–107
Growing vegetables 97–100

Hakonechloa macra 'Aureola' 133
Hand digging tools 57
    hand fork 57
    specialized bulb planters 57
    trowel 57
Harvest hazel (Corylus) 85
Hedera helix (Common ivy) 54
Hedera helix 'Atropurpurea' 39
Helleborus orientalis 85
Helleborus x hybridus 85

Hemerocallis 'Golden Chimes' 31

Herbs 116
  Bay (*Laurus nobilis*) 116
  Caraway (*Carum carvi*) 116
  Chervil (*Anthriscus cerefolium*) 116
  Chicory (*Chicorium intybus*) 116
  Chives (*Allium schoenoprasum*) 116
  Comfrey (*Symphytum officinale*) 116
  Coriander (*Coriandrum sativum*) 116
  Dill (*Anethum graveolens*) 116
  English Marigold (*Calendula officinalis*) 116
  Fennel (*Foeniculum vulgare*) 116
  Feverfew (*Tanacetum parthenium*) 116
  Flag Iris (*Iris versicolor*) 116
  Garlic (*Allium sativum*) 116
  Hyssop (*Hyssopus officinalis*) 116
  Houseleek (*Sempervivum tectorum*) 116
  Lady's Mantle (*Alchemilla mollis*) 116
  Lovage (*Levisticum officinale*) 116
  Meadowsweet (*Filipendula ulmaria*) 116
  Nasturtium (*Tropaeolum majus*) 116
  Parsley (*Petroselinum crispum*) 116
  Peppermint (*Mentha x piperita*) 116
  Red Orach (*Atriplex hortensis rubra*) 116
  Rocket (*Eruca versicaria sativa*) 116
  Rosemary (*Rosmarinus officinalis*) 116
  Spearmint (*Mentha spicata*) 116
  Sweet cicely (*Myrrhis odorata*) 116
  Sweet marjoram (*Origanum majorana*) 116
  Thyme (*Thymus vulgaris*)
  Winter savoury (*Satureja montana*) 116
Hesperis matronalis (Dame's Violet) 12
Hollyhock (*Alcea rosea*) 12
Hornbeam (*Carpinus betulus*)

13, 80
Horticultural fleece 87
House leeks (Sempervivum) 134
How plants grow 20

Ilex aquifolium 'Pyramidalis Aureomarginata' 29
Impatiens 136
Imperata (Japanese Blood Grass) 67
Improving your soil, how to 16–18
  double digging 16
  single digging 16
Indoor plants 49
Ipomea tricolor 'Heavenly Blue' 40
Iris reticulata 36

Laurus nobilis (bay) 133
Lavender (*Lavendula angustifolia*) 12
Lavendula angustifolia (Lavender) 12
Lawn mowers 59–61
  cylinder mowers 60
  rotary mowers 59–60
Lawns 124–31
  alternative lawns 128
  cornfield annuals 128–9
  creating a new 125
  feeding 127–8
  grass seed and turf mixtures 126
  maintenance 127–8
  mowing 128
  patching up 128
  perennial wildflower meadows 130–1
  quality turf, choosing 125
  scarifying 127
  sowing seed 126
  tining and top-dressing 127
  turf, laying 125–6
Leaves 22
Lewisia 134
Lobelia 136
Lobelia erinus 'Crystal Palace' 37
Lunaria annua 38
Lythrum salicaria 131

Mahonia japonica 'Bealei' 29
Making compost 17
Malus 'Evereste' 26
Marsh marigold (*Caltha palustris*) 137
Matteuccia struthiopteris 73
Microclimates 8–9
  shade 10

wind 9
Miscanthus 67
Miscanthus 'Ferne Osten' 34
Molinia caerulea 131
Monstera deliciosa (Swiss cheese plant) 55
Mulching 17
Myosotis sylvatica 'Blue Ball' 38
Myriophyllum verticillatum 42

Narcissus (Dwarf daffodils) 134
Narcissus 'Minnow' 36
Nepeta 'Six Hills Giant' 31, 87
Nerine bowdenii 134
Nigella damascena 67
Nigella damascena Persian Jewel Series 37
Nuphar lutea 42
Nutrients 18
  nitrogen (N) 18
  phosphorus (P) 18
  potassium (K) 18
Nymphaea 'Perry's Pink' 41

Opuntia robusta 46
Orchids 48
Organic matter 16–17
  adding 16
  composted bark 17
  farmyard manure 16
  garden compost 16
  hops and mushroom compost 17
  leaf litter 17
Ornamental grasses 33–4, 67
Osteospermums 23

Panicum virgatum 131
Panicum virgatum 'Rubrum' 133
Pansies (violas) 136
Passiflora caerulea 40
Pelargonium, *Chlorophytum comosum* (spider plant) 136
Pennisetum alopecuroides 'Hameln' 135
Perennials 30–2
Perovskia 'Blue Spire' 86
Pests & diseases 102, 105, 106, 107
  aphid 102, 106, 107
  blossom end rot 106
  botrytis mould 102, 107
  cabbage fly 107
  cucumber mosaic 102
  flea beetle 107
  onion root fly larvae 104
  parsnip canker 105
  red spider mite 102, 106, 107
  root aphid 102

slugs 102, 107
  whitefly 106
Petunia 136
Philadelphus 87
Phormium cookianum 'Cream Delight' 134
Phormium tenax 134
Photosynthesis 22
Picea orientalis 'Aurea' 27
Pinus mujo 'Ophir' 27
Plant adaptations 51–5
  epiphytism 55
  hot, dry conditions 51–3
  low light levels 53–5
  running, rhizomatous roots 54
  tap roots 53
Plant anatomy 20
Plant types 24–37
Planting alpines 74
  creating an alpine feature 74
  how to 74
Planting aquatics, 71
  in baskets 71
  planting deep water aquatics 71
Planting bulbs 68–9
  broadcast planting 69
  in a woodland setting 69
  in borders 69
  in containers 68–9
  naturalizing in grass 69
  new lawn 69
  scarifying 69
Planting cacti and succulents 72
  in containers 72
  outdoors 72
Planting climbers 70
  against walls, step-by-step 70
  growing through shrubs 70
  in containers 70
  obelisks and plant supports 70
  screens and dividers 70
  supporting and training climbing plants 70
Planting ferns 73
  soil preparation for ferns 73
  tree ferns 73
Planting perennials 67–8
  buying and planting 68
  for colour and height 67
  supports 68
  techniques 62–75
Planting trees & shrubs 65–6
  planting dos and don'ts 66
  watering in 65–6
  wetting agent 66

Plectranthus 136
Plumbaginoides 86
Polystichum setiferum 47
Pontederia cordata 41
Power tools 59–61
Powered hedge trimmers 59
Propagation techniques 89–95
  cold frame 90
  composts and compost
    admixtures 90
  growing from cuttings 92–3
  seed 90
  semi-ripe cuttings 93
  softwood cuttings 93
  division 94–5
  layering 94–5
  air layering 95
  plantlets 95
  potting on 91
  pricking out 90–1
  sowing seed 91
  tools and equipment 90
Propagator 90
Pruning & maintenance
    techniques 76–88
  bonsai, foliage pruning 84
  bonsai, root pruning 84
  clematis 83
  climbing plants 82–3
  hedges 80
  indoor plants 84
  roses 81–2
  trees & shrubs 77–9
Prunus cerasifera 113
Prunus spinosa 113

Pulsatilla vulgaris 45

Rakes 58–9
  landscape rake 58
  spring tine rake 58
Rhinanthus minor (Yellow Rattle
    or Hay Rattle) 130
Robinia pseudoacacia 'Frisia' 26
Root systems 20–1
  bulbs, corms and tubers
    20–1
  fibrous roots 20
  rhizomatous roots 21
  tap roots 20
Rosa 'Alexander' 43
Rosa 'Breath of Life' 44
Rosa 'Complicata' 44
Rosa 'Hyde Hall' 44
Rosa 'Little White Pet' 44
Rosa glauca 43
Roses 43–4
Rotary cultivators 59
Rubus thibetanus 'Silver Fern'
    135
Rudbeckia hirta 131

Salix alba var. *vitellina*
'Britzensis' 137
Salvia nemorosa 'Lubecca' 30
Sanguisorba canadensis 131
Sedum spectabile 'Brilliant' 74
Seeds 23
Sempervivum (House leeks) 134
Sempervivum 'Reinhard' 46
Shears 58

border shear 58
edging shear 58
hedge shears 58
Shrubs 28–9
Silphium laciniatum 131
Skimmia 134
Snowdrops (Galanthus) 134
Soil characteristics 18–19
  chalk soils 19
  clay soils 19
  loam soils 18–19
  pH, the importance of 19
  sandy soils 18
  silt soils 19
Soil type 15
Solanum pseudocapsicum 135
Species 24
Stems 21
Sternbergia lutea 134
Stipa gigantea (Golden Oat
    Grass) 33, 53
Stratiotes aloides 42
Swiss cheese plant (*Monstera
deliciosa*) 55

Taxus baccata (Yew) 13, 80
Taxus baccata 'Fastigiata' 27
Tilia cordata 85
Tools & equipment 56–61
  accessories 61
  eye and ear protection 61
  garden line 61
  garden twine 61
  gardening gloves 61
  safety 61

sprayers 61
watering equipment 61
wheelbarrow 61
Tree ferns (*Dicksonia antarctica*)
    73
Tulbaghia violacea 134

Understanding soil 15

Verbena 136
Verbena bonariensis 32
Viburnum tinus 133
Violas (pansies) 136
Vitis coignetiae 39, 85

Water gardening 137–42
  constructing a pond 139–40
  formal pond 138
  informal pond 138
  ornamental fish 142
  other fauna 142
  pond life 142
  self-contained water
    features 138–9
  water feature, types of 138
  water, keeping clear 141
Watering tips 88
Wellingtonia, *Sequoiadendron
    giganteum* 54

Yellow Rattle or Hay Rattle
    (*Rhinanthus minor*) 130
Yew (*Taxus baccata*) 13, 80
Your garden, assessing 8

Acknowledgements

The publishers would like to thank Coolings Nurseries for their cooperation and assistance with the photography in this book, including the loan of tools and much specialist equipment. Special thanks go to: Sandra Gratwick. Coolings Nurseries Ltd., Rushmore Hill, Knockholt, Kent, TN14 7NN. Tel: 00 44 1959 532269; Email: coolings@coolings.co.uk; Website: www.coolings.co.uk.

The photographs of the roses on pages 43–4 were kindly supplied by David Austin Roses Ltd, Bowling Green Lane, Albrighton, Wolverhampton, WV7 3HB. Tel: 00 44 1902 376376.

The pruning artworks on pages 109–11 were supplied by David Graham. All other illustrations were produced by David Etherington/Focus Publishing.